THE
Path
OF THE
Priestess

DISCOVER YOUR
DIVINE PURPOSE

co-authored by

ROSE COLE • JANE ASHLEY

ALI SHANTI/ALEXIS NEELY • ANNIE LALLA • ELAYNE KALILA DOUGHTY • JENA LA FLAMME

JENNIFER RUSSELL • JESSICA CORNEJO GALLEGOS • JULIE MCAFEE • SOFIAH THOM

Official book website: **www.thepathofthepriestessbook.com**

Published by:
Rituality Press, www.RoseCole.com

Book Creation:
Jane Ashley, Flower of Life Press™, www.FlowerofLifePress.com

Cover Art:
Android Jones, www.AndroidJones.com

Cover Design:
Jacob Arden McClure

First Printing 2015

Contents

Dedication

༺༄ ᐧ ༄༻

To all of the daughters who ever were, or ever will be.

100% of the profits of Amazon sales of this book are being donated to Pachamama Alliance,

www.pachamama.org

Our donations will be used to protect indigenous lands and to share Pachamama Alliances'
educational programs with people who are ready to take bold, effective action in the world.
Thank you for your support in this mission.

Acknowledgments

Thank you Nat Mundel, for not only fathering our daughter, the light of my life, but also for facilitating the growth and expansion that inspired my work in this book. And of course, deep bows of gratitude to my precious daughter Violet, for being my greatest inspiration, teacher, and muse.

~Rose Cole

A very special thank you to Android Jones for the use of his art, "Beauty in Perspective" on the cover and throughout this book. Learn more about Android here: www.AndroidJones.com

I am grateful for the support of all people involved in the creation of this book—thank you for saying YES with a full heart: Rose Cole, Ali Shanti, Annie Lalla, Elayne Kalila Doughty, Jennifer Russell, Julie McAfee, Jessica Cornejo Gallegos, Jena la Flamme, Sofiah Thom, Scott Watrous, Amy Paradysz, and to my children Ruby, Penelope, Annabella, Alden and Sadie. Without all of you, this book would never have been birthed into the world to do its work planting seeds of transformation.

~Jane Ashley

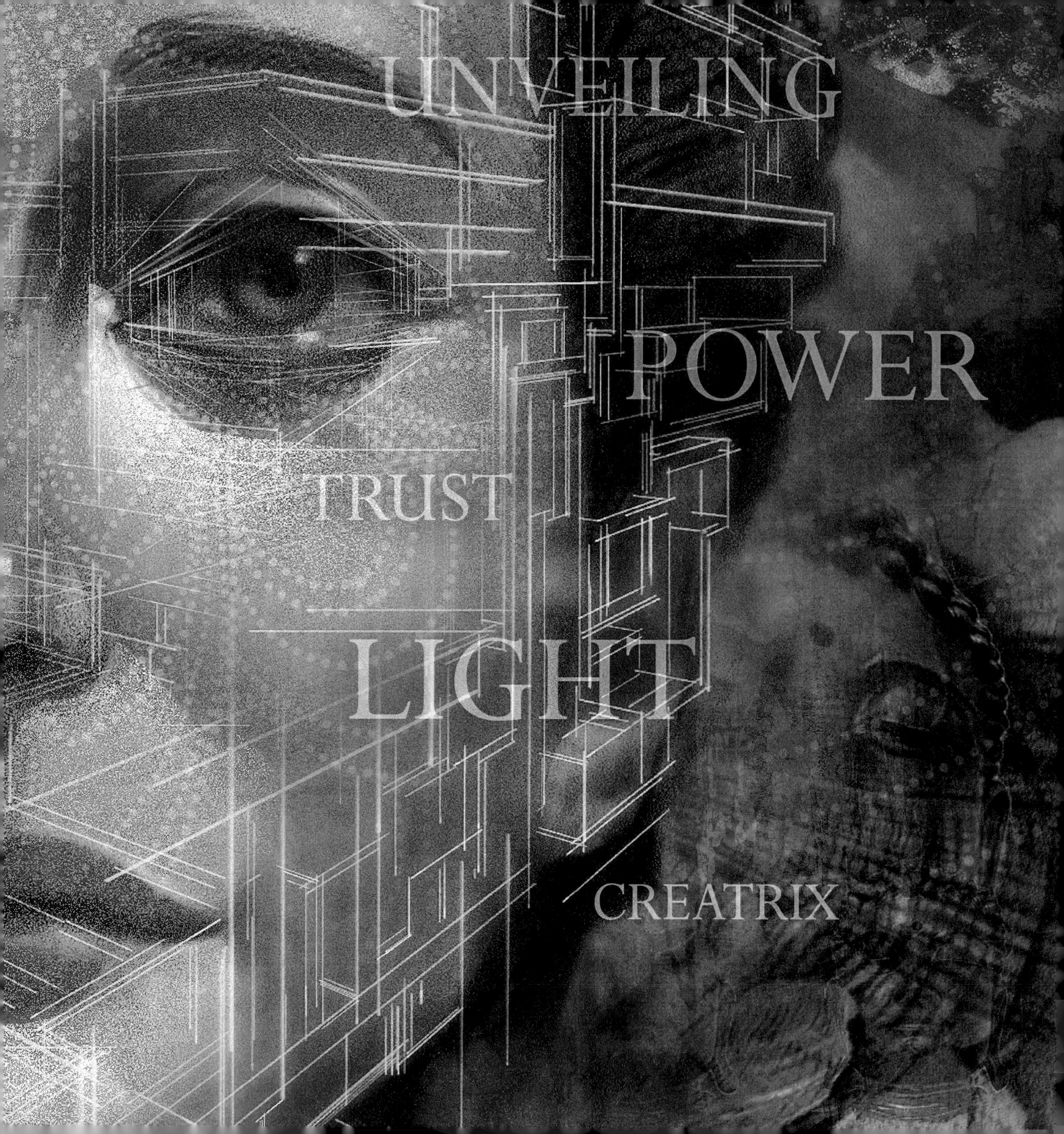
UNVEILING
POWER
TRUST
LIGHT
CREATRIX

Rose Cole

Chapter 1

RECLAIMING OUR POWER THROUGH RITUAL

BY ROSE COLE

It's December. My daughter Violet is in her car seat and I'm driving along the winding roads of my neighborhood in Rancho Santa Fe, California. She's a happy kid and this is a big day for her. We're on our way to a Winter Festival Fundraiser. She doesn't know it yet but today is going to be her first meeting with Santa.

She's laughing, babbling to me, and being the embodiment of adorable. I try to follow the logic of a two year old as we pass home after beautiful home in the fourth most expensive zip code in California.

I should be blissfully happy, right? This is what I wanted. This is everything I've worked for; a beautiful family, career success, and an overall great life…but right now all I want to do is leave my body. Outside everything is right but *inside*, there's a whole other story. Inside is pain, so much pain I'm not sure I can survive it. If a car hit me right now that might not be so bad—it might a good thing. If I die right now then I could just get some relief from the pain.

That feeling doesn't go away. I'm carrying it inside me even as my now ex-husband Nat calls angry at me for not taking him with us, despite my request for some much needed alone time to reassess our marriage and my life. Nonetheless, his emotional manipulation works again, and as usual, I did a u-turn and began the trek back to our house.

Keeping my cool with him demands the last little shred of energy I have. The normally calm and peaceful Rose began to slip through my fingers, and someone frightening to me emerged. I was a woman I hardly recognized.

We've all been there haven't we?

I hang up the phone. Everything becomes a blur as I race back home to pick him up and fight back the thought of driving off the road instead.

Red; I'm seeing red as I careen up the driveway, my energy so frantic and palpable that even Violet can sense it. It's only her tiny voice screaming "Stop it! Stop it! Stop it!"—a desperate plea to her mommy to come back to a normal state of tranquility—that momentarily snaps me into the present moment. Her screams interrupt a disturbing thought that is flashing through my mind: a twisted fantasy about ramming the car into the garage, over and over again. Of course, I would never do that yet when one is in such tremendous pain the mind can go to the darkest of places.

I slam the car door shut and storm up the front porch. The pumpkin sitting there doesn't stand a chance against my fury. I pick it up and smash it to the ground. It explodes in pulpy pieces all over the porch. This feeling inside me grows and is all-consuming as I fling the front door open, rage into the house, pick up the humidifier and hurl it across the room smashing that, too.

All I can think is: there's no more left of me. *"Will somebody, or something, please stop this pain?"*

I'm breathing hard. I'm spinning out of myself. Nat is there waiting, and I can see what he needs from me—that last little shred of attention and energy I still have left. And there's Violet, too. She needs me. *"Rose, you can do this. You can be there for Violet."* Nat brought himself along with his anger into the car and we made our way to the Winter Festival. I know the drill: once there, we were to become "the happy family." All smiles. Everything is fine. Isn't life grand?

The festival is a magical winter wonderland. It's San Diego, but there's snow courtesy of a snow machine drifting beautiful white flakes everywhere. Miniature horses are dressed up as reindeer and the smell of hot cider and gingerbread fills the air.

Family and friends are there so naturally I adorn a plastic smile. We begin the courteous small talk…about the kids, what's new, and the upcoming holidays. I pose Violet on Santa's knee and laugh at her curious reaction to this strange bearded man in a red suit. I make a gingerbread house with frosting and candy.

If only my life was as sweet as my surroundings. In reality, I'm just trying to hold it all together. It isn't just the constant anger, the emotional abuse and the disconnection that torments me. No, the pain is *much deeper*. The pain stems from unresolved issues around Nat's behavior that have been lingering for years, that I have allowed to happen. I was out of alignment; with my truth, my soul, my divine purpose.

Even with all my work to be a conscious and spiritual woman, I am having a *really* hard time holding a place of unconditional love for Nat right now. The happiness others see isn't what's going on at all. And all I can think is, "What the fuck? Me? *A High Priestess?*" "What *the hell* does that even mean anymore…High Priestess? Who the fuck am I to be writing that? Who am I to be working with women all over the world when my world is crumbling around me?"

There I was, the author of *High Priestess Training*, and I felt low. I felt like anything *but* a priestess.

I felt utterly alone.

Today, as I reflect back to that time in my life, I see I co-created a picture that was anything but pretty. I feel vulnerability and even shame over sharing this chapter of life with thousands of strangers. But that's the thing: life is often *not* a pretty picture. The truth is frequently ugly. It took months to work up the courage, but as I write this, I feel like I owe it to you to share everything. I want to allow you to peer behind the curtain and let you see what it really looks like to walk on the path of the High Priestess. We'll define that term in a moment.

First, let's back up. You see, all of that darkness didn't come out of nowhere. It started a month and a half earlier when I woke up to the realization that I had been normalizing unhealthy behavior I was witnessing in my own home. These destructive patterns and the resulting abuse led me to question everything I once held dear. The man I chose as my husband. My capacity to be a good wife and mother. My ability to make money and support myself. My credentials to be a spiritual leader and inspirational speaker. My basic human worth. *Everything*.

My lifelong passion for uncovering, living, and teaching spiritual truths had built a successful business. I attracted an audience looking to me for answers; looking to me for the path. From being on national television, to speaking in front of thousands of women, I

was known to others as *Rose Cole: Spiritual Leader.* I felt like such a joke! The uncomfortable truth was, during those dark and painful years, I felt like a fraud. If it wasn't for a small voice inside of me—a voice I learned never to censor—I may have never made it out of that living hell.

I'd been in the darkness before, but this time it was different. This time I wasn't blind-sided. This time I could see it coming at me and knew I had to make a decision. I could wait for it to swallow me whole or I could meet it head on.

I knew what I had to do.

I sat down and endeavored to explain it to Nat. I was going to elect to go into the deepest inquiry of my life and completely surrender myself to it. If I didn't I would go down fighting, or I'd have to rebury it. I'd never know what true surrender would bring. I knew for myself I could not go on living this lie anymore.

I asked Nat to hold space for me because I needed to question everything so I could reclaim my truth and re-align my intentions and my path. I needed to put every attachment in my life up on the altar. I needed to fall apart and then ask the Divine to put me back together. And I knew it was going to get very messy.

I asked for a month; a month to go into the darkness and come out the other side. I didn't know what that was going to look like but I knew the life I was living was not working and I would most likely have to completely deconstruct everything and rebuild it so I was in alignment with my truth. The pain was too big and this was the only sane option.

My only hope was that I'd come out of this with some wisdom I could share with others.

"Oh," he said, "you want me to *belay* you?" He used to be a professional rock climber and he explained *belay* was a climbing term. *Belaying* is when you're free climbing and you have someone spotting you with the rope that's ready to catch you if you fall. *"Holy shit, that was exactly it!"* I thought.

"Yes," I told him, "that's what I need."

I had another question: "What happens if you're climbing a huge mountain wall and you see the top. You really want to go there, but you're too paralyzed, comfortable, or scared to take it all the way?" Nat said, "There are a few things that could happen...You can climb down from where you are but the problem is it might take twice as long to climb back down and you might not have enough food or supplies OR you can put all questions about not getting there out of your mind and just go for it."

"And if I just stay there, right in that same place on that wall?" I asked.

"Well, then you're clinging to the side of a mountain, paralyzed with fear. Eventually your muscles give out and *you have no choice but to fall.*"

I had suffered many metaphorical falls and broken bones in my life even before I knew I was on this path of the Priestess. I knew he was right. This time there was a sense of where I was on the mountain...but did I had the confidence to look up to the top and see it through?

Nat agreed to a month of time and space for me to explore where I was on this mountain called life. So I decided to go for it. Climbing into the darkness, into my insecurities, my doubts about myself, my feelings of shame, and the truth of what was happening in my home.

I knew when I finally reached the summit that I would be stronger, clearer, and in alignment with my truth. I also knew I would discover some wisdom to share with other women, but that didn't make any of this easier. This was going to be harder and scarier than anything I'd ever done.

What prompted this dark period was a realization I was out of integrity in every area of my life. The house I was living in and the pretense of a perfect relationship. *"I'm a spiritual and lifestyle mentor! How could I have normalized such unhealthy patterns in my own life and relationship?"*

I allowed myself to completely fall apart. I questioned everything in my life, my identity as a wife, a mother and spiritual leader. There were days I looked into the mirror and didn't recognize myself. I was like a caterpillar who'd gone into a cocoon. Caterpillars don't just sprout wings, they first completely digest themselves with the release of an enzyme that reduces them to a thick goo. *I became the goo.*

To understand myself and find a path out of this darkness, I had to go back to where it all started: my childhood.

I grew up very poor, in a home with lots of abuse and trauma. I never knew my biological father and my mom wasn't always emotionally available. My stepfather was bipolar. When he and my mom weren't selling drugs they were using them. There was no one in that house reading me bedtime stories, helping me with my homework or making sure I brushed my teeth. I slept on a mattress in the corner of my room, with no sheets, a thin

My old neighborhood, Clairemont, CA.

blanket, and a foot of trash. Every night was terrifying. Oftentimes, no one paid attention to where I was or what I was doing. Despite all of this, I was a happy child. I was in touch with the spiritual side of my life for as long as I could remember.

All of that changed, seemingly overnight. It wasn't until recently that I understood why a once-bubbly child turned into a depressed and withdrawn little girl who, at times, literally wanted to die. The reason: at the age of five, I had my power robbed from me. I was sexually molested by our neighbor and I repressed this memory for several decades.

Clairemont, the San Diego suburb I lived in then, was the opposite of Rancho Santa Fe. It was a place created with so much promise, San Diego's largest postwar suburb. A new concept in community living—not based on the grid system—with winding streets meant to take advantage of the canyon views. The reality was quite a bit different. The green lawns had turned brown and the single-family ranch houses looked worn out and broken down.

This is the house I grew up in.

It was a spring day, and I was outside playing, when I realized I needed to pee. I knocked on the door of our neighbor, Bob, and asked him if I could use his bathroom. He was the friendly, "grandpa" type. He let all the little kids swim in his pool. It seemed okay when I knocked on his door, but as soon as the door closed his whole demeanor and energy changed. I watched something very dark and sinister come over him. He pinned me to the bed, and jammed his fingers inside of me.

It was painful. Traumatic. I didn't think he was ever going to let me leave. I was powerless and terrified I'd never get home. And to my utter confusion, there was a sexual awakening inside of me. I now realize I had what's known as a *kundalini awakening,* a primal energy normally awakened by healthy sexual or physical encounters. I left my body and hoped I would never come back. When I did return, all that remained was the darkness, the blood, the horror, and the shame. A very protective part of my little brain decided in that moment to bury this experience until the day arrived where I could process and integrate it into my being.

The signs that I had been molested had always been there. When I became pregnant I had so much anxiety around the exams and such a fear of the internal workings of a woman's body my doctor had asked me if I'd ever been molested. Therapists had asked throughout my life, too.

Going into the darkness forced me to look at this memory head on and see how it had impacted every part of my life. When that man put his hands on me, sexuality and fear got all tangled up. The result was that I couldn't have an orgasm or get turned on unless I subconsciously replayed the event. I became fascinated by older men. They were scary and repulsive, but also a turn-on.

Then one day, it all finally clicked. When that man put his fingers inside me, wiping my blood on his pants, my five-year-old self felt that I was bad, shameful and dirty. It reminded me of my own filth; my skirt, stained with ketchup and left unwashed by my mom. It was filthy. I was *filthy*. I *was* a dirty little girl, and now this stranger put the ultimate exclamation point on how truly "dirty" I really was.

There was only one way out. I had to prove to the world that I was worth something—that I wasn't dirty.

I had to prove that I had class. But this wasn't going to be easy. The wounding of my childhood had just begun.

In the years that followed, my mother and stepfather went through a horrific divorce. My mom had several nervous breakdowns, which led to her not being able to care for me anymore. I bounced around from home to home and don't really remember entire *years* of that period of my youth.

I finally landed at my aunt and uncle's house. Can you imagine the mindset that such a tumultuous childhood would produce? I didn't think I had any worth, I had zero self-esteem, I was terrified of the world and didn't think I could do anything on my own.

I was highly empathic and intuitive, making me overly sensitive to other people's energy. On top of this, I knew that I was an outsider in this new place. Kids made fun of me and adults felt sorry for me.

It was then that I set out on my journey to find "class". I started to study people that were popular, had money and what I thought were good upbringings. I started to model what they did: dressing like them, doing my makeup like them, behaving like them. I desperately wanted to fit in.

The house where I was molested at age 5.

What I didn't realize until shortly before my dark night of the soul was how much this belief and survival mechanism was still at play in my life. Here I was, buying the "right" clothes at fancy stores, all name brands the world would recognize and that promised me "class".

The decision to live in Rancho Santa Fe stemmed from the same thing.

I'd built my own business and become a successful entrepreneur to get to this place. Here I was with Nat, who came from an upper middle class East Coast family who hunted. And along came my adorable, blonde haired little daughter.

I had finally made it. *And almost all of it was a lie because I was living out of alignment with my truth and Divine Purpose.*

The biggest tragedy of that day, what I call an "Essential Event", was that I learned I couldn't trust myself. An Essential Event is the moment in time when your consciousness is fragmented, and your ego is formed. *All of the Karmic patterns you came to break here in this lifetime*

10

are created. This is your first heartbreak or betrayal and it usually happens before the age of seven. As tragic as your Essential Event can be, I believe it's one of the primary reasons we come into and experience humanity.

By looking at the patterns in your life, you can follow the cosmic breadcrumbs back to your childhood. From there, you can see where they originated from, decode them, and integrate them into your being. This is not always a pretty path, but once you spot your Essential Event and resolve it into your being, you change the energetic vibration raising it to a higher level. This will attract people, things, and events into your life that are more of a vibrational match to your true essence and higher purpose.

For example, the day I was molested started a long-standing pattern of giving my power away to men. When I knocked on that door, every cell in my body said, "Something's not right." I went in anyway, and ultimately learned not to trust myself and my inner knowing.

I created a soul contract in that moment: that I would never be a perpetrator like this man was. So instead, *I became a victim.* He touched my g-spot—the pleasure center of the body. After that, whenever anything felt too good or I felt too much pleasure in any area of my life, the alarms would go off, "Something bad is going to happen."

When you are living out of alignment, the voice trying to gently usher you back onto your Divine path gets louder and louder. Eventually, the voice becomes a scream, and anything shy of prescription drugs, shopping sprees, or constant distractions momentarily turns the volume down.

That universal voice was screaming at me for years, and I turned a deaf ear to it. Now, I was the one screaming…screaming back at life. But now, I was ready to breach the summit. I was ready to take the next step. I had the mountaintop in my sights. I knew I had to make peace with my Essential Event; to integrate it fully, once and for all, and to share this wisdom and peace with women everywhere.

Thanks to the Power of *Rituals*, I took the final steps. Now, I am standing on that summit. Before me is the most beautiful vista; a breathtaking view of a world full of inner peace, happiness, and abundance. A world without "class", because the need for the false appearance of class has melted away…

On the summit I stand alone, yet I am embraced by the Universe. The same is true for YOU.

Those of us on the High Priestess Path know that once you invoke being on this journey, our very compassionate universe won't let you off the hook. It's easy to forget when we are presented with the opportunity to grow, it is *we* who were the ones who asked to go to the next level. The next level is achieved by using the gift of rituals.

Rituals have been used for thousands of years in every indigenous culture around the world and are important rites of passage that have almost been forgotten by modern society. They're also a way to bring things to completion. I define a *ritual* as anything we do with intention. They mark a moment in time where we are choosing consciously to stop the karmic patterns replaying in our life.

Rituals are medicine for the soul.

When we have something incomplete it takes up space in our being. If I hadn't taken action, the voice telling me everything was wrong would just keep getting louder and louder. I could now see that who I was attracted to and chose as a husband was because I was attracting the match to my unresolved karmic patterns. This is very important. I knew I would keep attracting these destructive patterns into my life. So in order to reclaim my power and learn to trust myself, first I created a ritual.

Rituals don't have to be elaborate: writing stream of consciousness thoughts down on paper and then burning it, throwing a rock that signifies something you're ready to release into the ocean, stepping through a threshold…All of these simple acts can become rituals if they are done with *intention*.

There are a few reasons why people don't create rituals. There's the fear that they won't keep a ritual up and be disappointed in themselves, and there's a fear of "doing it wrong." It's not about perfection, it's actually *doing* it that matters.

The intention in *doing* creates the magical thinking that allows us to release space in our being. This empowers us to create an opening for love, happiness, wealth and other positive experiences to enter into our lives. When the ritual is complete, there is an immediate shift. You can feel the change that has taken place inside your body.

This process can take anywhere from days to weeks, depending on the amount of clearing that needs to be done. Those old thoughts and habits will still come creeping up. It might even feel like it didn't work. These feelings are referred to as an *echo effect*. It's the echo of the old pattern reverberating.

It might feel easy to embrace the echo and go back to your old patterns but what has actually been manifested is an opportunity to prove to yourself that a change has been made. This will allow you to move into deeper levels of growth.

When faced with an echo, stop the train of thought and consciously pivot in a different direction, letting your mind move towards the new way of being that you are creating. Also, allow yourself to feel gratitude. Gratitude is one of the most important emotions to cultivate when re-aligning yourself to your Divine purpose.

The rituals healed my deepest wounds, allowed me to re-align and took the form of several steps. My first step, was to get a sitter for Violet so I could take Nat to the house in Clairemont where I lived when I was five. This was huge. It was terrifying for me to show him how poorly we lived. On that visit, I was in touch with all the shame I had felt, never wanting anybody to really know who I was or where I really came from. There's a picture of me from that day. When I look at it, I can see all the pain and darkness I'd been feeling, but I can also see my intention.

The next step was the journey to the house where my Essential Event took place. I stood in front of the house and told Nat exactly what had happened there. I saw a sign in the driveway "Bob parks here." A shock wave went through my body as I realized the man who molested me still lived there. In an instant, I was that five-year-old girl all over again but I stood my ground as tears started to roll down my face while I continued my story. I felt the shockwave roll through my body and leave. That dark energy I'd held inside was released and I could feel something within me shift…I was reclaiming my power and my inner knowing.

I had taken the first crucial steps in ritualist form in order to reclaim my power. However, there was one more ritual to do.

I went to the beach at Mission Bay playground where I used to play as a child. I found a long crack in the sidewalk. To me, this sidewalk represented the timeline of my life and that crack was a threshold I was about to step through. When I stepped over that crack I stepped into the rest of my life where I could now live as my authentic self. This sounds so simple, yet the effect was utterly profound.

That day, in that moment, the darkness vanished.

Creating that simple set of rituals and facing my biggest fear allowed me to shed that other life and begin to step into my power. While rituals mark the moment in time where we take a stand for the end of the karmic pattern, this is when the work and the unraveling of the karma actually begins. Just because you create a ritual doesn't mean all of your problems disappear. It means you are invoking help and support in putting a stop to the karma and patterns you are ready to shift. This ritual for me began a process of completely dismantling all of the constructs I had built that were no longer serving me.

Now I live life radically, on my own terms and without apology. My life is my own. I may be eccentric and offbeat to some. I might even be considered wild. However, my life is my own…and to be honest, *I kick ass*. Stuff still comes up, but I am now attracting very different things into my life.

This is the way of The High Priestess Path. It's about finding the radically unique path that is yours and yours alone. It's about breaking the paradigms and karmic patterns we've individually chosen to come into and to transmute them into Divine power. It's about looking at the problems in your life and saying, "Okay, I can take you on, I've got this".

Those of us in this book and on The High Priestess Path know we're on the tip of the spear. We are blazing a trail, and showing others how to break out of the mold, find your truth, and create a life you love that is completely your own.

As you've now seen, this process is messy. This path is littered with the bodies of those who have caved under the pressures of family, society and our own expectations. But that's why you're here, reading this book. That's what this book is about: women like me, letting you peek behind the scenes by sharing our real, authentic selves.

So, my advice is to hold onto your panties. We're laying it all out for you and we're not sugarcoating anything. You'll experience the good, the bad and the ugly. This is what *real life* really looks like.

We aren't saying this is the path you should take, but we *are* saying this is a path that can give you hope. It's going to be messy, like it is for all of us. You're going to have doubts and fears, but you're ready to shout… to live out loud!

You're here to be a leader in a consciousness revolution that's happening at this very moment in time.

It's true: you're going to have to ruffle some feathers. You're going to have to figure out your own truth in order to radically and fearlessly live it to the fullest.

And that's okay. That is what it means to walk The Path of the High Priestess.

Welcome your rituals, as we, the women who are your sisters, welcome you.

"The essence of my teachings is rooted in sharing with others the miracle of incorporating simple and uplifting daily rituals into our lives. These rituals serve as an opportunity to come back into our hearts, re-anchor our awareness in the present moment, align with our deepest intentions, and create a life that is continually attuning and harmonizing with our soul's highest truth."

About the Author

ROSE COLE

Through Rose Cole's personal journey and the challenges that she's overcome, she's discovered how to manifest and create the life of her dreams. From a thriving and fully self-expressed career, having her beloved daughter, to the beautiful home and incredible community of friends and colleagues that she gets to co-create life with every day, Rose has found the path to fulfillment. It's a deeply soul-fulfilling joy for her to share with others a system of practices that she calls 'Rituality', which have been such a powerful and inspiring force in her own blossoming and transformation process.

Rose is a visionary leader and world-renowned speaker, co-author of 'Audacious Aging' alongside Deepak Chopra and Dr Andrew Weil, Shamanic Priestess, popular featured guest on TV networks such as E! and MSNBC, and preeminent mentor and spiritual guide who has helped thousands create thriving and awakened lives.

She's also a leading luminary in a new paradigm of heart-based entrepreneurs who are dedicated to embodying their highest potential: body, mind and soul, and illuminating the path for others to do the same. Rose's path has been one of transcending adversity, trauma and several 'dark nights of the soul' in order to harvest the wisdom, strength and perseverance that such adversities inherently bring, and to share the power of possibility to benefit as many people as possible.

Rose is also the creator of **RoseCole.com**, a website filled with articles, videos, and resources for living a more fulfilling life. Please visit **Rosecole.com/FreeGift** today for your free High Priestess Training video and audio series.

For more information about how you can work with Rose, booking inquiries and press requests, please contact: **info@rosecole.com.**

Chapter 2

SEEKING THE TRUTH IN THE LIGHT AND THE DARK

BY JANE ASHLEY

My dear sisters, I invite you to settle in, get comfortable, and open your heart to receive the energy in this book.

We are convening now to hold hands in our circle of sisterhood and hold the vibration of love, together. We are here to create change, to wake each other up, to honor the Divine Feminine inside of each of us, and our Mother Earth. We are here to plants the seeds of change to bring more love and light into the world. We are here to serve each other and our planet in love.

As the creator of this collaborative book project, I want to share with you how this idea came through me, how I received the information, and then the tumultuous process of birthing it into life. This process—the creative process—required that I peel away all of the layers energetically that bound me to the rules I was taught to follow, step into my power, love myself, release inner darkness, and keep evolving in every moment through all of it—love *and* fear, light *and* dark. I really had the hardest two years of my life—and at the same time, I have become a completely different person, accessing a whole new level of self-awareness and knowledge of how life works. This project has been a portal into the next level of my evolution. I have learned how the creative force—my essential life force—is most important to tend to as I grow and change.

I now walk the Path of the Priestess.

I always had a sense that I was different. I remember as a child feeling like I was stuck inside my body looking out at the world around me, like there was a glass wall separating me from the rest of the world. I was often angry and couldn't figure out why. It felt like there was a whole lot of dark lurking around inside of me—and I couldn't find my way through it.

As a young girl, I put myself in risky situations. At age 5, I stole a snack from another child's lunch in kindergarten. I once stole a piece of candy from the grocery store (it was unfortunately actually a cough drop) and got caught. I was mortified as I handed over the sticky lozenge to the clerk, who looked at me like I was the devil incarnate. I cheated on a test in 2nd grade. Got caught. More shame. Why was I doing these things? I felt like such a bad girl—broken, incomplete, damaged. Now looking back, I see that I was giving myself a big dose of shame everytime I acted out.

One time, I was running really fast in the house, and then I threw a heavy knob from the coffee table because I wanted to test how powerful and strong I was and see how far I could throw it. But when I broke a glass vase and got in trouble, my belief that I was a "bad girl" was completely validated. *Don't be too powerful or you'll get in trouble and be a bad girl.* So I became a rule follower. I stayed small, did what others wanted me to do, and didn't trust my inner voice. I deferred to other peoples' opinions. I stayed small and hid my power away. Who wouldn't make the choice to stay small in order to not make a scene and get in trouble? For a little girl, it makes sense that I would develop certain coping mechanisms so that I could learn to fit in and feel safe. However, as an adult, hiding away from my power definitely did NOT serve my highest good.

This powerlessness was a self-fulfilling prophecy that manifested later in my relationships, my sexuality, my health, my emotional well-being, and as panic attacks where I would hyperventilate and have to breathe into a paper bag. My body was definitely trying to tell me that something was off.

Even through navigating the dark times, there was a lot of light and love in my life, too. On my 10th birthday, I twirled around in the grass, looking up at the sky, and felt connected to GOD—to the bigger power, to the Oneness of All that is. It was a breakthrough moment of wonder and love that flowed through me and imprinted itself. There were more of those

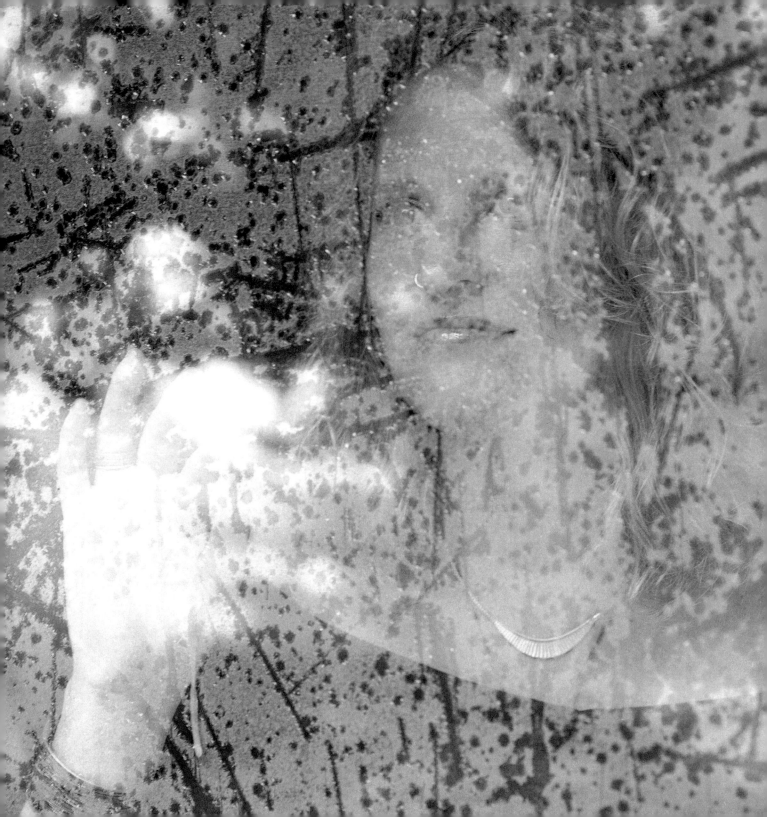

moments of being dipped into Big Love, but I seemed to always get yanked back out again into more struggle. The search for that love continued on.

As a child, church felt like just another thing that my family did for socializing. I didn't feel any connection to a "God" or higher power. In high school, I attended a Christian retreat through my parents' church with other teens—a few of them from my school. While there, I again experienced an overwhelming sense of spirit and GOD's presence. I felt the power of love, friendship, and trust, and for the first time since twirling in my yard at age 10, I felt the higher love taking refuge in my heart. It was an amazing feeling! So much expansion! This is what that familiar phrase, "God is Love" was really all about.

Unfortunately, once I returned from the retreat and was back at school, I felt like I'd been manipulated, deceived—brainwashed, even! Where was the love and community, now? My classmates who had also attended—who I had opened my heart to—were suddenly nowhere to be found. Somehow, as a teen without any follow-up from that weekend retreat, I was unable to perpetuate the feeling of connection and love that I had experienced. It was gone and I was right back to where I'd started. I felt abandoned by the kids and the retreat organizers. It just affirmed to me that if there really was a God, he was not a nice one. I got depressed. I ended up getting a job in a restaurant and never went back to church again. I stopped thinking about God. I was pissed at the whole idea. *The notion of GOD is total bullshit.* From that moment on, I convinced myself that I was an atheist. My heart clamped down.

Now when I look back, I notice patterns in my life of depression, internal conflict, negative voices, poor self worth, and a closed heart. I was shut down with an impenetrable wall around my heart. Even when others tried to help me with my unhappiness or anger, I didn't want to go there—my life was just fine, thank you very much! Yes, I thought I was happy, but I had no authentic feeling inside of self-love. I didn't even know there was a heart space inside of me that needed anything! I felt very numbed out emotionally—like an ice queen. Of course, to me, this felt normal.

By age 35, I had achieved a level of success that looked to the outside world like I had everything together: a degree in Graphic design, status-filled jobs in NYC, a masters degree in Counseling Psychology and Art Therapy, a job as a therapist at Yale, a loving husband, 3 beautiful daughters, a house near the beach…I was living the "perfect" life.

I had no idea my life was about to completely blow up.

I realize now that my first marriage was doomed because I was emotionally shut down, numbed out, and disconnected from my own divinity. Critical inner voices were screaming at me all the time but I kept that volume turned WAY down—muted, in fact. It was all there under the surface but I just couldn't see that my shadow self—the stifled, pissed-off little girl inside of me—was the one who was *really* running the show.

How could any one really love me when I couldn't love myself?

Then, in 2008, my perfect life came crashing down when I fell in love with someone else—whom I later married. Talk about self-shaming! Boy, was I was a bad girl *now*…burning down my "perfect" life, hurting the people I loved, wallowing in "poor me"—I felt like the woman with the Scarlett letter on her chest. I was so angry and hurt that all my girlfriends had shunned me—or so I convinced myself. In fact, the reality was I shunned *them* out of *my* own shame, but could never consciously allow that to be true, so I created an experience of victim for myself. Just another reason to keep that glass wall around my heart.

When I got divorced, I began to rebuild my life and start the healing process. I knew I needed to change so I could be the best mom to my daughters and not pass this baggage down to them. I feared I'd fail them and they'd end up in therapy for their whole lives! I'd been to therapists over the years, and I was a damn good therapist myself! *So good for other people, but no good for me.* I had empathy for everyone else but me. My relationships had the scent of inauthenticity about them. I had no idea how to let love in. No therapist could help me discover what was really going on deep inside. I knew I had to try a different approach because I was a master at staying on the surface, never diving down into the depths of my soul. It was too scary. But something new was propelling me forward. Something different. I felt like my soul just grabbed my hand and started running—sprinting!—dragging me behind and forcing me to take a long look at what I had created in my life.

When I discovered Rose Cole's program *The Powerful Woman Powwow*, I went through a process that allowed me to finally get out of my own way and find my way back to the remembrance of who I *really* was and always had been. I broke through and landed in GOD space again. Three days of intense work in a circle of supportive sisters felt like I had done 30 years of traditional therapy!

Yes!!! This is what I'd been searching for! Boom! In an instant, I was experiencing ecstatic bliss and was filled with the Purest Love. My heart cracked wide open and love flowed in. I had never felt anything like it. Even my childhood experience swirling in the grass, and the experience of love at the church retreat couldn't come close to what I had discovered…*I am part of All that is. I am here for a purpose. I am child of the Universe—of GOD.* I had power and light and love rushing through every cell of my being. I was made of Divine light! I *was* love. I remembered.

Thus began the work of sustaining the remembrance of this truth. I made a choice to really love myself no matter what and stop judging myself. I stopped caring what others thought of me. I was finally autonomous.

Without knowing what I was doing, I had stepped fully onto the Path of the Priestess.

Walking this Priestess path is not easy. It requires being acutely aware of and willing to catch every single negative thought or low vibration in my system, and say to it, *"NO! You are not welcome here! I desire to stay in the light and be in the vibration of love!"* On this path, there is no end point, no final destination, no where to get to. It's about choosing to release so much "DO-ing" (very masculine energy) that we as women we are so well trained in, and instead balance it with the "BE-ingness" of life (very feminine energy). It means accepting all parts of myself, just being me, and honoring the sacredness of my life and my conscious-ness. It means feeling my life force flowing and buzzing under my skin. It means facing the darkest moments and embracing each moment with gratitude. It requires witnessing my life and not letting emotions or reactions take over. Being present. Grounded. Aware. In forgiveness for myself and others.

In every moment we have a choice—to go light or go dark. Here is *my* secret—BE HERE. NOW. BE PRESENT. All we have is this moment! What are you going to choose in each moment as your life unfolds? Will you choose to be reactive, irritated, angry, miserable, or sick? Or will you choose health, love, abundance, joy, the energy of creation, and being supported?

I know how easy it is to stay miserable. At the beginning, it was *hard* to keep my higher self in the drivers seat. But as I practice staying present and catch those shadowy thoughts in each moment, I find it much easier to stay in a loving space. Love feels so much better and brings better results—it is the highest vibration there is. I just keep reprogramming my thoughts so that I believe it.

Presence is a tricky word to understand with our brains. Meditation helps me understand what it is, because when I meditate and notice all the runaway thoughts in my mind, I have an opportunity to dis-identify with them as my truth and replace them with a new belief or thought that serves. It allows me to empty out the static in my mind and rest in silence—in the space of pure creative potential.

> *Sit.*
> *Breathe.*
> *Listen.*
> *Keep listening.*
> *Catch the thought!*
> *Release it, and come back to the breath.*
> *Start again.*

This practice can be difficult to sustain, though. It takes diligence to go inward to catch those thoughts and replace them with something more positive and loving. What works for me is to practice presence *off* the meditation cushion and in my daily life. I continue to do it even as I carry out mundane tasks like grocery shopping or doing laundry, or when running my business, taking care of my family, and hanging out with friends. Every moment requires precision so I can choose the path of love and light. When I emanate love, I feel pleasure in my whole being. This pleasure I receive from staying open-hearted makes it all worth it. It is the juiciness of life!

But hey, don't worry when you find yourself on the dark side of the coin—no judgment, here. The dark is a gift! It is our teacher. It is the portal to understanding what we need in order to choose the light. When you finally climb out of the dark space, even if it's days later, you can remind yourself, "Oh, yah! That was just me choosing the dark path again! Now I can choose the *light*—more LOVE." So you flip it. Reprogram it. Choose a loving thought, instead. Find your way back to your open heart that intuitively knows how to give and receive love.

Since that cosmic reintroduction to my divinity back at Rose's house in 2009, I have sought and experienced true sisterhood. I have fallen in love with the Divine Feminine in myself and in all women. There is nothing like the joy of sharing energetic space with women who love you unconditionally, who are also committed to the Work. Radical responsibility is required to clear out the stories in our system so we can live our Divine Purpose here on this planet—

collaboratively rather than in competition. I am blessed to have discovered a tribe of conscious women who also walk the path of the priestess. They inspire me!

Now, my creative flow has opened up, I have grand visions for my life and I manifest what I desire. I receive information and downloads as creative ideas and projects and fully trust that there is a purpose for me to bring them to life—for myself and for others—especially through books. This is my Divine Purpose.

In 2013, I again sat in ceremony with Rose and many of the sisters in this book. At one point, I felt a bolt of energy and light run straight through the top of my head and land FIRMLY in my heart. In that moment, I had a realization:

I am here to usher my own voice and my sisters' voices, messages, and vibration out into the world. I am here to love the Divine Feminine in all women. I am to be a beacon of light for others to remember their own divinity.

When I returned home and shared this realization with my husband Scott, he planted the idea in my mind for this book.

I am to midwife a cutting-edge, collaborative book project about Priestessing out into the world to sow the seeds of transformation and evolution.

Thus began the creation of the book you are reading.

Through the process of writing this book, this group of authors has experienced it ALL— the good, the bad, and the ugly! Myself and others have been dragged through the muck. Lives have changed, deaths have occurred, divorces have happened—Dark nights of the Soul galore! It has truly been like a Shamanic Journey to pull us all together in collaboration. We have received the gifts of our own transformation as we prepared to speak our truth and send it out. We have experienced an abundance of love, peace, joy, bliss, and sisterhood. We have had to wait, be patient, release blocks and fears, travel down into the depths of hell in our personal and professional lives, too. We have had to rise again like the Phoenix, stay determined, continue to forge forward and create. We have had to soften our hearts to ourselves and forgive. We are shadow walkers *and* light walkers—two sides of the same coin. Both are gifts, both are our teachers. As women who follow the path of the priestess, we seek truth in the light AND in the dark. We confront our fears and bust through for the sake of *all* women.

This book is like a baby and we are *all* her mother. She is her own entity. She has an energy that contains the collective energy of all of the authors, and she also carries her own essence— that of the Divine Feminine. Now, we pass the baby to you. We trust that she will serve as whatever medicine you may need, in the highest service of all. And so it is.

"I have always seen the world as a canvas, and my education as a psychotherapist and as a designer centers on merging emotion and form, layers of texture and energy merged into a statement of visual essence. I write the words and paint the picture that takes form in my heart, defining my clients with truth and their own reflection, and then mid-wifing their books and message out into the world. I am many other things besides a Brander and a Publisher—mom to 5 kids, daughter, sister, wife, friend, and daughter-in-law. I believe in the power of sisterhood, and I am totally committed to honoring the Divine Feminine in each of us, and holding the highest vibration of love for ourselves and the planet. That is my calling. Being a Publisher is a dream, and a responsibility. I am ready."

About the Author

JANE ASHLEY

Jane Ashley is the Publisher of *Flower of Life Press* and is the creator of this collaborative book project, "The Path of the Priestess: Discover Your Divine Purpose". Jane holds her Masters degree in Transpersonal Counseling Psychology/Art Therapy from Naropa University, and completed Nutrition training at the Institute for Integrative Nutrition. She was a featured guest speaker at IIN's 2012 fall conference at Lincoln Center in NYC.

Prior to starting Flower of Life Press, Jane was the Creative Director for the Globe Pequot Press, a book publisher based in Guilford, CT., where she managed a team of 8 award-winning designers and was the creative leader for the company in the US and in the UK. While there she art directed the New York Times bestselling books *Crazy Sexy Cancer* and *Crazy Sexy Survivor* by Kris Carr. Some of Jane's former clients include TimeWarner, Inc., the McGraw-Hill Companies, Amex, FedEx, IBM, as well as many successful coaches and wellness professionals. Jane know the hurdles in launching a business, finding time for self-care, being with family, and the importance of collaboration in this new economy.

Her passion is to help women elevate their consciousness, lives and businesses—by distilling their essence and creating a deep emotional connection through their message—to a place they never dreamed possible, while breaking through perceived barriers to find joy and purpose in their lives.

Learn More: **www.floweroflifepress.com** or email: **Jane@FlowerofLifePress.com**

Ali Shanti/
Alexis Neely

Chapter 3

THE PRIESTESS PATH: TAKING THE ROAD LESS TRAVELED

BY ALI SHANTI / ALEXIS NEELY

*"Do not follow where the path may lead.
Go instead where there is no path and leave a trail"*

~RALPH WALDO EMERSON

The Priestess Path is not for the faint of heart. It is the road less traveled.

While the path is not an easy one, it is the most rewarding journey I've ever been on personally. I have no question it will be the same for you. As you step onto the path, you must be prepared to allow everything that is not your truth to burn away. This burning away process can feel painful, confusing and lonely at times. In the most challenging moments, take comfort from knowing that you are not alone. You are being held in a Sisterhood of the highest order.

We are waiting for you to emerge out the other side of your personal alchemical process and join us in the ever expanding Good that is unfolding here in the hidden spaces of our consciousness.

Allow my story to be a guide for your journey.

My path began as traditional as you can imagine. Straight from college to Law School. In my last year of Law School (1999), I got married on Valentine's Day to the man I began dating when I was twenty, pregnant a month later, graduated summa cum laude (first in my class) that May and off to Florida to begin my clerkship with a Judge on the 2nd to highest court in the land that August. My daughter was born in November of that year.

A year later, I was firmly ensconced in one of the best law firms in the US. Earning $160,000/year, commuting twenty miles each way in Los Angeles traffic, leaving my baby with her dad, who had agreed to be the stay-at-home parent, day in and day out.

I was twenty-eight years old and had achieved everything I set out to achieve in my life up until that point. Married, check. Great job, check. Baby, check.

My heart was breaking. Could this really be it? Was this my life for the next sixty years? The loneliness invaded my soul like black ice spreading across the highway. No one could see it, but it was there, lurking and dangerous, waiting to derail the best laid plans.

I had the job everyone wanted, but it wasn't for me. It took hiring a coach I thought I couldn't afford and a near death experience to realize, I am an entrepreneur. I can't work for someone else. I have to start my own law practice.

Everyone told me I was crazy to think of giving up my big law firm secure paycheck after just three years to start my own law firm. But, crazy was apparently my path because I did it.

I started my own law practice in 2003 and after a year of struggle decided to do another crazy thing and focus the practice nearly entirely on serving families with young children. Everyone I spoke to told me I would starve. They said families with young children didn't want to think about death and estate planning. And, if they did, they wouldn't pay for it.

I knew they were wrong and I went for it. By 2006, my business was bringing in over a million dollars a year in revenue. I was so glad I followed my intuition and didn't listen to the naysayers.

It happened again during my divorce. All the lawyers and most people I spoke to said I should take my husband to Court, not give in to the fight and hold out for him to get close to nothing.

I decided to do the opposite and give more than I thought I had, ask him what he needed in order to be safe and say yes to paying him $4,000/month in child support and alimony.

I didn't have that money at the time, and I believe it's a big part of why I was able to build a million dollar practice, quickly. Where most people would have contracted so they had less to give, I expanded and created more for all of us.

Fast forward to 2009 and I had sold my law practice and built a second million dollar business, this time training other lawyers on my unique practice model. In addition, I had another business with my life partner, at the time, serving entrepreneurs to bring their businesses online.

I had written a best-selling book, appeared on all the top Television shows, including the Today Show, Good Morning America, O'Reilly Factor and more. The pinnacle of success.

And, yet, more than anything, it felt like a trap.

There was a part of me longing to get out and I couldn't understand why. I had achieved the success we have all been primed to want. Why did it feel so bad?

I constantly heard from my team "Alexis, you can't do that. Alexis, you can't say that. Alexis, you can't wear that. Alexis, you can't write that. Alexis, you can't be that. You'll hurt the business."

But the business was hurting me. I was working constantly to keep up. My business model was off and I knew it wasn't sustainable. I was burdened by all the people depending on me to keep earning money in ways that no longer felt in alignment with my truth. But I didn't know what to do.

I had built a business that looked amazing from the outside, but inside I was dying. While I was surrounded by people, I was so lonely. The people in my life didn't feel like friends, they felt like people who were around for the money.

Once again, I couldn't imagine doing what I had created for myself for the next forty years.

So, I decided the only answer was to give it all up. The brand, the reputation, the image, the fans, the followers, the likes, the support staff, the income.

It was a two year process of letting go, one step at a time. Until, finally, I was living on just $5,000/mo (down from $70,000/mo), on a farm, in a very small two bedroom farmhouse with no Xbox, no television, no housekeeper, no personal assistant, no one to cook for us, no one to grocery shop, and no one to drive the kids to school.

It was time for me to step up and discover, "Who am I if I'm not a money maker? What do I really want? How do I create a life that is in alignment with the truth of who I really am?"

I drove my kids to school each day. I grocery shopped. I cooked. I swept the floors and made the beds. I played cards with the kids. I launched a weekly show called the Whole Truth Show. It had no business model. Just me and my friends, hanging out on camera and connecting with my online community for four hours every Tuesday.

People thought I was nuts.

But I kept asking the question, who am I really? What do I really want? And then I followed my desire, no matter how weird it looked.

Ultimately, what came through is that I did want to continue serving lawyers. I did want to make money again. And a whole new understanding of the way we make personal finance decisions that keeps us enslaved to a system that doesn't truly serve.

It turns out that what I missed the most when I lived at the farm and what I promised to add back in as soon as I began making money again was the support of people in my life who I was paying. What was most funny about that is that resistance to supporting people who were working for me was one of the reasons I decided to shrink. I felt taken advantage of, used, put out, burdened and overwhelmed by all the people who had been depending on me for support.

So I withdrew, shrunk and pulled back. What would happen, I wondered, if all the people I was supporting financially stopped receiving my financial support. Would they disappear?

Some did. But most, didn't. In fact, they showed up more. Finally, there was space for my ex-husband to support me. I began to recognize that most of the people in my life weren't there just for the money. They were there because they loved me and they were my family.

Once I got that, I also understood my role in the ecology. My entrepreneurial archetype is that of a Star Creator. It's the highest leverage, highest income earning role in the constellation of the Entrepreneurial Archetype map. The Star Creator also employs the most people.

As I made the decision to come back into the world and begin earning money again and rebuilding the businesses that would support my work, I made a commitment to do it differently.

Alexis Neely

Ali Shanti

Today, the businesses that support my work once again earn more than $2,000,000/ year and employ more than twenty people. This time though, I not only don't feel burdened, but I feel consistently grateful AND I am just one part of the team that makes the machine of my home and the businesses run. I no longer feel as if I have to do it all alone.

And, I no longer feel as if I am on a quest for financial freedom. Instead, I've found the path I now understand (and teach) as financial liberation. I know what I need, how to earn it by providing tremendous value in the world, in alignment with my Truth and I'm rewarded for taking the road less traveled.

That's the one thing that has never changed.

While I was living on the farm, I discovered the part of me that had been longing, craving and screaming to come out.

Her name is Ali Shanti. My name is Ali Shanti. And, it's also Alexis Neely.

You see, I've discovered I have many parts living inside me and these two, they both like the spotlight. They both want to be seen. They both have Great Work to do in the world.

Alexis Neely is the part of me that graduated first from law school, trains lawyers and is a hardcore, badass business babe. Ali Shanti wears feathers, speaks at festivals, and it turns out is a badass business babe herself, but in quite a different way.

I live fully out loud as both of these parts of myself today.

People told me I should stop. I should "kill off" Alexis Neely. I should hide Ali Shanti. Just pick one, they said. Integrate. You are appearing fragmented. It's confusing. Really, you should stop doing that.

But, I couldn't.

The Priestess Path is the road less traveled. Even when it looks unusual, awkward, uncomfortable, confusing or weird to others, I knew the right thing for me was to be all of myself. Out loud. Fully and completely.

The most amazing thing is that the more I take this road less traveled, the better business is, the more people I serve, the more people I meet who know me and want to get to know me more.

My most recent path has led me down the road to creating a public blog in which my (now former) partner and I were posting publicly the most intimate details of our relationship.

Our relationship came to a transition point because I want to be open, non-monogamous, polyamorous, call it what you wish—I want to have sex with whoever I want, whenever I want. I am taking on sexuality as a spiritual path.

And I write about it publicly.

Again, many have said, "Alexis, don't do that. Do what you want, but keep it under wraps. Do you have to be so public about everything? At least wait until you've resolved the questions you are posing. Don't be so damn messy."

That's not my path.

My path is to live out loud. My path is to share what's raw, real and true, as it arises. My path is to live my life as performance art. Fully open. Revealed.

My path is the Priestess Path.

UPDATE: Since writing this piece, a year has gone by. The relationship I began writing about publicly has ended (quite publicly), and I've gone through yet another transformation.

Today, I am in a deep process of integration. Over the past year, I came to see that my two personas were created because I didn't fully accept all of myself and I created these two distinct versions of me as the first stage on the path to full self-acceptance.

The next step in that process is the re-integration into a single whole. My true self.

This work of integration is requiring me to face anything and everything that is not truth within me and in any of my relationships and transmute that lack of truth into a higher energy.

Often, this looks like ending relationships, letting go of team members, making choices that feel really hard, but actually create so much ease once they are made and the resistance is dropped.

In the time since I wrote the initial piece, it feels as if I've been down the road to hell and back again with my 15-year old daughter, and can honestly say today that I'm parenting totally unconventionally, but we are both happy and trust each other, which feels monumental and so good.

I'm in a new relationship today that is likely the healthiest relationship I've ever had With an amazing, conscious, quite younger man (19 years younger, for those who are counting), who absolutely adores me. And who I am discovering what it really means to love with.

I wish someone had told me earlier that getting into relationship when I am not in full self-love is simply a recipe for pain. For all involved. Today, my self-love is reflected back to me in the eyes of my partner. And, yes, we are exploring "open" relating, though it looks far different than I imagined open-relationship looked before.

Internally, this road less traveled often feels incredibly scary and I wonder if I can keep going, but generally by the next day, I've regained my footing.

Again and again, I come to remember that on the path of the road less traveled, the bumps in the road still exist. And, it is these very bumps that are the spice of life. They are what keep life interesting and why I incarnated in this physical form. My desire is not to smooth out the path and settle for mediocrity within a range of safety. My path is to glide through all the ups and downs with as much grace as humanly possible.

On the road less traveled, you will see it all, experience it all, feel it all and your job is to face it all, welcome it all, say yes to it all. Be with it all. The path of the priestess. Keep saying yes. To all of it.

Full range is the name of the game. Keeping your eyes and heart wide open.

Feel. It. All.

On the road less traveled.

Welcome, sister. You are home. We've been waiting for you.

"I took the road less traveled by, and that has made all the difference."

~ROBERT FROST

About the Author

ALI SHANTI / ALEXIS NEELY

Alexis Neely, who you may also know as Ali Shanti, is a new economy personal finance expert who offers a fresh perspective for personal finance and business decisions. She graduated first in her class from Georgetown law and quickly scaled the ranks of "successful" entrepreneurship before recognizing that she was compromising her greatest gifts in the name of "success". Since then, Ali has discovered her own unique genius is in guiding you to discover yours so you can fully contribute to the co-creation of the dream so many of us are dreaming.

Alexis has built multiple million dollar entrepreneurial endeavors both online and offline, wrote a best-selling book, appeared on numerous top-rated television shows, and today lives a new economy life in community with her ex-husband, kids and extended chosen family. She shares her transparent journey through the ups and downs of finding herself so you can do the same.

Alexis's two current business ventures, New Law Business Model and Eyes Wide Open Life, both fully location independent, provide new economy business model consulting to people who want to serve others deeply, living their own unique genius and make a great living while they do it.

Alexis is based in Boulder, Colorado, but is location independent and travels frequently, attending and speaking at festivals and conferences, and her teams are also location-independent or "digital nomads" based mostly in the US and Canada.

Check her businesses out at **www.eyeswideopenlife.com** and **www.lawbusinessmentors.com.** Follow Ali herself at **www.alialexis.com**

Annie Lalla

AVATAR OF LOVE

BY ANNIE LALLA

I'm running down the street barefoot. Everything whizzes by in a blur. My heart is racing but my thoughts are in slow motion. I weave between a moving yellow cab and the curb, wondering what could happen if I let it hit me. It doesn't but I'm startled by the near miss. Being so close to death reminds me I'm alive.

I look down at my naked feet, toes painted pink. I don't know why I'm here, what I'm doing or where I'm going. Shame slides edgewise into my heart as the insanity of my situation settles in. Tears and confusion well up in my throat. How did I get into this crazy mess… running barefoot through NYC to escape a boyfriend I'm convinced is trying to kill me.

My name is Annie Lalla and I'm a Love Coach.

As a relationship expert, I help people communicate their feelings effectively so they can find and keep True Love. I show clients how to build their self-esteem and attract the highest caliber life partner. Here is the story of how I almost lost my one chance at True Love.

I believe romantic relationship is a portal to self-actualization. Being in love is a spiritual path. It's the place you are forced to excavate your darkest shadows and asked to fulfill your potential by becoming the most extraordinary version of yourself. We all need a mirror to see our blind spots. Our partner is that sacred mirror.

But like all things sacred, True Love is shrouded in mystery. The journey is equal parts excitement and terror. If done right, you inevitably enter a process of annihilation. The individual "I" is forced to die into a "We." That's why it's scary, and why we resist it on pain of death. It's not always apparent, but the "We"—when cultivated with fierce commitment—gives us back an "I" vastly more expanded than the one "sacrificed." But few romances live to tell this truth.

True Love is not for the faint hearted, it's a gladiator sport. Many give up when it gets too hard. But once you're actually in Love, you simply cannot leave; there's nowhere else to go. Like an exquisite trap it holds you tight, binding you to growth.

True Love is the only force strong enough to keep you in the game when everything else says run. Anything less, is a brand of settling, where "good enough" dresses up as The One. I'm great at finding would-be sell outs in love, because I came so close to selling out on myself.

Here's what happened: A few years ago, I was dating a true gentleman—a brilliant psychiatrist with a PhD from Columbia University, top of his class. We quickly fell into a deep romance. Within three months he was ready for marriage, kids and a nice house in Brooklyn. At 38 years old, I was very tempted. He was smart, handsome, sensitive and treated me with reverence. I loved him dearly, but something was missing

In retrospect, I see how much of our connection was funded by my primal reproductive imperative. Getting older had me anxious to make a baby—and he could feel it. His readiness for that future was very compelling. On some unconscious level I was interviewing for a baby-daddy rather than looking for my soulmate. I couldn't see it clearly at the time but I was actually selling out on True Love for the incessant ticking of my biological clock—a common blind-spot in aging women.

While we were dating, I was a fully-fledged love coach. My clients adored me and thought I'd found my True Love, which of course inspired them. I remember thinking, "If I break up with him, the world will think I'm a total fraud—no one's ever going to trust me." How could I support others if my own relationship failed?

In some ways, I got better at my work during this period. I could easily smell the indicators of any client's potential selling out—because I was living it. Despite a low-level unease with my relationship, I kept squinting at my doubts and let the affair go on for months. I met his family, he met mine. He even 'secretly' bought me a wedding ring.

But there's only so long you can keep a lie to yourself. In my deepest heart, I knew we weren't a match. There was a subtle, but ever present question, "Is he the one?" That incessant uncertainty is what finally clued me in. *My hack: if after a year of dating, you're still not sure, then they're not the one. If you think you may be settling, then you are.*

When our soul finds its mate, that particular question disappears. You go from "Is this going to work?" to "How is this going to work ?"

What finally allowed me to make the painful and heroic shift out of that relationship, were the powerful insights I gleaned from a deep meditative journey.

During that journey, I had a vivid, surreal and traumatic dream vision. My boyfriend and I were sitting in my apartment, talking about our future—marriage, kids, the whole thing—when suddenly I began to panic. Terror rushed through me, inchoate fears began to spin into private hysterias. I shared my distress but everything he did in response reduced my sense of safety. As my emotions intensified, I quickly descended into a bottomless paranoia, which sent me darting full speed out of my apartment, terrified he was going to "kill me."

Barefoot and petrified I raced down three flights of stairs while visions of blood flashed across my mind. I ran my fastest, never looking back, for fear he was chasing me with a knife. I found myself hurtling through the streets of NY desperate for help. Nowhere was safe, I felt alone and afraid. Four words kept looping inside my mind: "I'm going to die. I'm going to die. I'm going to die." That's when I noticed the yellow cab and wondered if jumping in front could end the terror.

Eventually, I found my way back home and the visceral nightmare subsided. With some space, time and processing, I realized the whole experience was my subconscious trying to tell me, "Your spirit is going to die if you stay in this relationship. Your purpose, your mission, everything you stand for is going to die."

During that journey, I woke up to the painful but undeniable fact that I was selling out on my most valued belief: True Love is real and possible for me, no matter how old I was. My animal had been choosing a "good enough" baby-daddy over a sacred soulmate. This was in such defiance of my truth. Some wise part of me knew the moment I stopped believing in True Love would be the moment I stopped wanting to live. My very identity was tied to this belief. To sell out on that would cost not just my happiness, but my very soul. I saw how close one can come to a silent, cynical betrayal of what we hold dear. I almost defiled my most sacred truth. And if I could do it, anyone could.

Soon after that, we broke-up. I made a clearing in my life and a pact to my self. I stopped looking for the father of my future child and instead committed to finding the man I could love forever, baby or not.

Two weeks later I met someone in a dusty tent at the Burning Man art festival. He was speaking to a large group of people about leadership, describing the future and explaining how the success of the whole world depended on the success of each individual. I was instantly smitten. He would go on to change the definition of what "man" was for me. His name was Eben Pagan and he turned out to be the love of my life.

That's when my whole story—indeed my entire life—shifted.

But I almost missed meeting him in the first place. I woke up that fateful morning at Burning Man with my entire camp going to hear some semi-famous marketing guy (Eben Pagan) do a talk. At the time, I thought sales and marketing was smarmy, so I opted out of going. Two hours later, I leisurely walked over to pick up my friends. As I entered the tent I saw the "marketing guru" at the front. He was still talking, but strikingly handsome; so I sat down.

To my surprise, he wasn't speaking about business or marketing. He was giving a heartfelt invocation for each of us to wake up and discover our unique gifts, then bring full attention to honing those powers. Until each of us actualized our individual skills, the species as a whole—he claimed—could not get to the next level. I was in awe.

Powerful, articulate and passionate, I felt him speaking directly to every un-manifested dream in the room, especially my own. It was the most inspiring talk I'd ever heard. And from that moment on, my heart was abducted into Love.

I had many ways to categorize men. There were smart men, good men, bad men, nice men, interesting men, worthy men, sexy and shady men. But he didn't seem to fit into any of those labels. I was forced to create a new category just for him.

Imagine all the fanciest cars you know: Rolls Royces, Mercedes, Ferraris and Lamborghinis, they're all amazing but Eben was an intergalactic vehicle like the Starship Enterprise. He was a whole different class of space/time machine—going where no man had gone before.

On some level I knew I'd fallen in love. On another level, I just felt starstruck. I had cultivated the ability to chat and flirt with intelligent men, but this encounter had me paralyzed and silent.

My girlfriends walked over to him after the talk. I hovered nearby, deathly quiet, way too shy to speak. They bantered back and forth, then he gave us all his email. I took the piece of paper—like a sacred object—and knew once I was at home and calmer, I could reach out to him online. The rest of Burning Man, all I could think of was Eben.

He was smart, he was handsome, he was making an important difference in the world. But what really pulled me in was the earnest congruence in his demeanor. I'd never seen anyone do marketing or sales that didn't seem shady, but he felt authentic and honest. His intentions were immediately trustable.

I initiated an email dialogue, hoping to pull him in closer with clever writing. My deepest insecurity is about my intelligence, so I overcompensated by turning up my intellect in hopes he'd fall for the 'smart' girl.

Turns out he was already dating someone, and despite being envious of her, I didn't try to undermine their connection. Instead I offered myself (being a love coach) as a sounding board for any of his relationship issues. One weekend while Eben was in NYC, I hosted a party with some friends at my place and invited him and his girlfriend over. They were having some relationship drama, so I sat and coached him (the man I wanted to marry) on how to be a better boyfriend to this woman. When you love someone, you love them whether they're with you or not.

His relationship ended a month or so later, and I continued to connect with him via witty and flirty email dialogues. But I wasn't the only woman in his life; he still had a cadre of ladies he saw periodically. Despite sharing a vast array of philosophical interests and epic conversations, he did not recognize me as his future mate. I was but one of the girls in his rotation. At one point, Eben confessed he wasn't very good at relationships and didn't even believe in True Love. He claimed he'd given up on the dream of a life-partner…alas.

I kept trusting that eventually he'd realize there was something cosmic between us. It isn't easy knowing the man you're in love with is off on a date with someone else. But we weren't in any official relationship, and I figured he just needed time to see how compatible we were, so I trusted in the process. One of the reasons I was willing to wait, as long as it took, is because I knew on some deep level that I would love him better than any other woman ever could. This is what gave me the courage to be patient. Besides, once you meet the most extraordinary man you've ever known, there's nowhere else to go. It was impossible to settle for less, now that I knew he existed.

One evening, while staying with him in LA, Eben suggested we go out to dinner with another lady he was dating—let's call her "yoga-girl". Since he'd given up on ever being in love with one woman, he wanted to have the two main girls he was dating meet in person, so everything would be less secretive and complicated. Being very open minded, and feeling confident in my ability to meet Eben in a future partnership, I agreed to go on this triple date.

She was very sweet over dinner, we all talked and hung out for a few hours back at his place. But throughout the evening I started to sense he had more familiarity and rapport with her than with me, and I could feel my heart beginning to break. I observed subtle cues—like where he chose to sit, how often he touched her, the amount of attention he gave her and by the end of the evening, I realized that he wasn't with me, he was with her energetically.

As the night progressed, my fantasy of being his future partner slipped away. Nausea moved through me as I realized my dream was turning into a nightmare. A familiar terror crept into my psyche, with that same haunting mantra in the background…"I'm going to die. I'm going to die". At some point during that night, a part of me did die—it had to. The Annie that was desperately in love and looking for him to love her back died. She died into LOVE itself. It was then that I realized what True Love was—the willingness to keep my heart open and stay committed to the connection even (especially) while going through the deepest heartbreak. When you're really in love, them loving you back doesn't change your affection. "It is an ever fixed mark."

A part of you must die into True Love; this is both terrifying and necessary. It's an initiation into the most elite club available to human beings.

I felt everything that evening—from fear, to anger, to relief—but I surrendered to the situation as it was because I loved him.

There's a fine line between loving someone and truly being Love, where the conditional lover dies into the unconditional one. Yet, across that line lies a vast chasm. My friend John Perry Barlow says it well: "The difference between Love and True Love is the difference between a very large number and infinity."

That takes courage and audacity; something I would learn more about the next day.

But back to the romantic drama.

Two women with one man—there definitely was jealousy on both sides. There I was, sitting in Eben's apartment while the 'other' girl (my competition) was garnering more of his attention.

But we each kept it hidden. That's how jealousy rolls (like shame and envy), always hiding it's tracks and often in the guise of anger. I could tell she was agitated and didn't want to go home and leave him alone with me. Suddenly all her 'emotional issues' starting coming up, I knew she was bidding for more attention. Noticing his commitment to helping her through her own emotions, I stayed on his side and actually ended up coaching her and him through some intense drama for about two hours—secretly fighting back heartbreak and tears the whole time.

Once she calmed down it was so late she just stayed over in his bed. Her on one side, me on the other, Eben in the middle. Nothing happened, everyone was exhausted and seemingly asleep. I didn't sleep a wink. I lay there comatose, sobbing secretly as my dreams crumbled inside.

Eben thought everything was fine with me because I'd put on a strong face of being "supportive" all evening. Inside of course, I was totally heartbroken. The other girl left early before Eben woke up, for yoga. By morning, I had finally let go of the idea that we were ever going to be together. I knew I loved him, but he was not choosing me. So I decided I would simply be the best friend possible by trusting and encouraging his life choices.

The next day, I couldn't hide my pain and for the first time, upon his inquiry, I shared my raw feelings. Since I'd already surrendered to us not being together, I somehow allowed my trembling heart to come forward and express my disappointment. Through streaming tears—without blame or make wrong—I shared how hurt I was at observing his preference for the other girl. I admitted directly, "I really, really like you, I don't think you realize how much." Then I started to cry. It was the first time he'd ever seen me show any vulnerable emotion and it affected him. In a sudden surprising resonance, he shed some tears as well. He was so sorry to have hurt me.

It turns out, he had no idea I was in such pain; I'd covered it up so well. It was an amazing experience to see how much he cared about my feelings. Eben explained, that to him, I seemed so composed and resourced while the other girl was upset and shut down, that he put his energy on making her feel safer, instead of me. With my seamless facade, he never once thought I might be hurting. In that one conversation, I felt his heart touch mine directly and a new level of intimacy emerged. Soft and empathic, he persuaded me to stay one more day with him.

Having now given up the attachment to him being my soulmate, our interactions became more fluid and tender. I was coming from a deep place of friendship with no mating agenda and that allowed me to relax into being fully expressed and real.

That whole day we unfurled in riveting conversation. We exchanged our most granular world views, debated philosophies, shared our future visions and discovered even more beauty in each other. It was engaging, expansive and immensely fun. I felt so free I realized I wanted to tell him my whole truth. In the middle of the day—as a charming anecdote for our new friendship, I revealed that I had been in Love with him this whole time. And after giving up on us being in a romantic partnership, I still loved him but was willing to support whatever romantic choices he made. I expressed this new truth with such ease and grace, I think it landed with a congruence that shocked him.

He was totally bowled over in disbelief. Something about my unclenched unattached assertion unlocked a door in his heart. I told him earnestly, "I love you, I'm in love with you," with no expectation of reciprocity in my voice. And instantly I knew, he heard and believed it.

For the first time in my life, loving another was not contingent on anything, especially not on him loving me back.

We spent the entire day trading insights on a sofa together, up late into the night, and at some point when I was least expecting it, he said, "I see you Annie. I recognize you as the one I've been looking for my entire life. You're the one." I recall that exact moment with dizzying glee. Every experience in my life seemed to lead up to this. It was, is and will likely be the most ecstatic moment of my life.

The next morning, Eben wrote an email titled, "I Found Her", to his friends sharing how he'd finally discovered the woman made for him…and it was me. There I was, inside my biggest dream come true. It was so real, it was surreal.

One of his friends wrote back immediately asserting this must be a joke…April fools etc. They mostly assumed 'someone like Eben' would never fall in love.

But they were wrong. The man I saw speaking in that dusty tent at Burning Man, the man that I instantly recognized as being my soulmate, had finally recognized me as well.

A man who firmly did not believe in true love, marriage and children is now married, deeply in love and the soulful father of a delightful 2 year old. We named our girl "Love", so that we could be "in Love" forever.

Before you assume this is some sort of happily ever after story, know that it's been the hardest relationship I've ever known. I have never fought, cried, howled and stood at the edge of my sanity as much as I have in the last 5 years of our romance. If happiness is what you're after, True Love is *not* for you. You'll feel it of course, often…and at a level that will flatten whatever you know to be ecstasy. But True Love is your ticket to fulfillment, deep soul-level joy, not the transient ephemerality of happiness. It contains within it every possible emotion—from euphoria to terror, from delight to despair. If you want to feel the most alive, so alive that at times it will feel unbearable, then this is the game for you.

In the end, I found my life partner—the man who'll be at my side for the rest of my life. And that makes all of it worthwhile.

As human beings we are fallible, imperfect creatures. Our wabi-sabi messiness is what makes us unique and irreplaceable. Yet we ache to be more than we are, good enough never is. All neuroses and insecurities stem from our knowing we're going to die someday. Death is the mother of all fears.

However, when you know you're loved completely by a partner that chooses you anew every day, your existence ceases to be empty or meaningless. It provides indisputable proof that you matter, deeply. Every moment you meet your lover's heart in that sacred house of US…you wake up into magic, you feel omnipotent, you taste eternal life. And those are moments we measure our life with.

True Love can also offer immortality in the form of a child that carries your imprint into the future. Creating a successful human being is the most romantic project a couple can undertake. And when the parents are in love, the child feels it's own body as a testament to that love, producing the esteem of someone who knows they deserve a magnificent life.

Love also keeps us from going mad. We all have some secret form of insanity that courts us incessantly. Sanity can come from being in love, because you have at least one other person "in here with you"—creating a shared reality that keeps you tethered to this world. When there's a safe place to be our full self (which is what a Love relationship affords) we can finally fulfill the sacred purpose we came here to do and leave our legacy. This is another form of immortality.

Within the crucible of True Love you can fully realize your greatest gifts, and generate the courage to contribute them to the world before you die. In a way, our entire species depends on you actualizing your full potential. We need you to hone your unique super powers and become your highest self. And romantic relationship is the ultimate context for that existential imperative.

True Love is the most powerful answer to death, emptiness and madness. I invite you to take it very seriously. Believe in it as if your life depends on it. Because it does.

About the Author

ANNIE LALLA

A thought leader, speaker and teacher, Annie is known as the "Cartographer of Love". She's spent her life mapping the subtle complexities of communication in romantic relationships.

Annie has created a suite of practical tools to help her clients resolve toxic patterns, increase romantic esteem, defuse conflict, assuage shame/blame and cultivate deep, resilient relationships that last a lifetime.

Specializing in love, sex and conflict resolution, Annie shares her signature method: 'The Art of Fighting'. She sees conflict as a crucial part of developing intimacy. "Arguments are opportunities to understand your partner better. When handled with curiosity and skill, they can pull you closer rather than apart."

With an Honors Degree in Human Biology and Philosophy (minor in Buddhism), her studies include integrative psychology, evolutionary science, therapeutic sexuality, and family systems dynamics. She also has professional certifications in NLP, Coaching and Hypnosis. All these realms converge in her unique Relationship Coaching practice where she helps individuals build extraordinary connections that maximize freedom and minimize shame.

Learn More: **www.annielalla.com.**

Chapter 4

I AM HER VESSEL:
WALKING THE PATH OF PRIESTESS PRESENCE

BY ELAYNE KALILA DOUGHTY

I am Sigune—
Grief Woman.
I am here now:
surrender, receive,
trust, release,
open to all faces of love,
light and shadow.
On the other side of loss is honesty.
I am a priestess of the flame.
Vessel lit in Holy Mother's name.
I am Her presence.

Somewhere deep inside the darkness there is a spark of light that is growing. Somewhere deep inside I am being indelibly changed from the inside out. Somewhere deep inside, in a place I can feel but not see, a mystery is unfolding. I am dying. I am being born. The woman I am is dissolving…but I am not. I surrender, I receive, I trust, I release.

This feels too naked. I know I signed up for this Priestess Presence path. I know I said I was willing to walk my talk, to heal my own wounds in service to the collective. But you want me to go *here*? You want me to open *this* space? You want to me to not only go through this but to *share* it?

Yes, beloved, I do. Open; share what's real, not the sterile contrived story. The vulnerable, tender quivering one.

And so, I am here now, braiding my heart's threads of shadow into words.

Come, sit a moment with me. I need you to be here with me.

Let us go slowly.

Let us look into each other's eyes and take the time to see who is here.

I want to see who you are beyond your name and personality. I want to feel your heart beat next to mine as we share the triumphs and losses in our lives. I want to sit and drink tea out of my favorite bone china cups and light a fire to warm us as we sink below the surface. I want to hold your hand to my cheek as I share my heart. I want to feel the pulse of our life force and know that this moment is sacred. I want you to feel how your presence soothes my soul, how you are a great gift. This is what I want.

I want to dissolve the barriers that would keep us apart. I want to be in *presence* with you. I want to share my heart with you.

In refrain, I want to hear your heart song. One heart beating.

This is not *my* story, but *our* story, being spoken through my body. Your body. Our body. We are *Her*.

I bow to you, beloved one.

In the quiet of this moment, I let my words seep slowly on the page, like tender and coy secrets I am quivering to share.

I will tease them gently like precious gifts. Not merely words, but expressions of my humanity, clothed in letters. These words hold my deepest love, my tears, my grief and loves, and my greatest light.

I am Sigune,
Grief Woman
—Queen of Death—
holding the portal between the worlds,
where loss is love and grief is liberation.
Come with me.
I want to share a sacred secret place with you.
It is about as intimate as I have ever been with anyone:
that is the point.
I took the sacred vow to walk the path of Priestess Presence…and
I must be willing to go to the places that scare me.
This is my chance to embrace
the dark, silent, shadowy places that hold all the light.
Shhh, let's tread lightly for all our hearts are here.
Our secret places are here.
All that is most tender, most human, and most precious lives right here.
Come in.

I am forty-six years young. I am "way over the hill," as they say, where I come from. And yet, as I stand looking down at the words PREGNANT I feel my whole being light up. Of course, I do what any woman like me would do: I run back to bathroom and take another test; I mean there must be a mistake, right? But the second and the third tests reveal the same simple truth: PREGNANT., I am completely overjoyed. My heart leaps, my womb vibrates, and tears roll down my cheeks. "How is this even possible?" I hear my own voice saying. I am laughing, crying, and shaking. I have never been pregnant and I have never used birth control. I did not think this possible. I had convinced myself 15 years ago that this was not possible. *I was not able to have a child that was that.* It was, very simply, not *my* path.

This is a miracle. A miracle is "a highly improbable or extraordinary event, development, or accomplishment that brings very welcome consequences." Yeah, that's it.

Somewhere, in the darkness deep inside, life is taking seed. As my belly grows—as I feel life take shape in me—I am birthing myself. As a baby is conceived, so a Mother is born. I am beginning to crack apart. The story I have told myself is flaking away like old skin. NOTHING can prepare me for the unfolding mystery.

You see my love, I had a story—a very convincing story that I had been telling myself for the better part of my life. It went something like this: "I am at peace with the decision to NOT have a baby. I have chosen not to be a Mother to my own child. I am here to Mother to the world. I have worked this through, thought it through, felt it through, done my therapy. I am in a conscious decision." This story felt safe; it was so believable that I hid within it for decades.

And now, with the seed of life growing inside my womb, my baby taking form inside, this nice, tidy, secured story began to shatter.

Mother cried:

"Kali-Eh-Swaha! I cut through all of your lies and illusions!
You have THOUGHT this through?
You *do* get that this has *nothing* to do with *thinking*!
You cannot reduce the power of life, the majesty of conception,
the mystery of incarnation to a mere *thought!*
HA, You THOUGHT it through."

I rallied back at Her "Yes!" I know this is the first sign of denial, but I felt so righteous—I really *did* do my work on this!

Through my twenties, I was too messed up to think about having a child. And, frankly, being around kids brought up untold rage and anxiety. In my thirties, I vacillated and tried to reconcile my lack of maternal instinct and "decided" that Motherhood "was not my path this lifetime." It felt true; I had never fell pregnant, never used birth control, and so clearly the decision was being made for me. Besides, by the time I was thirty-nine, I married a woman…so getting pregnant was REALLY not an issue. We all agreed that the ship had sailed. Done and dusted. Phew…

Only it had not.

Somewhere in the darkness, deep inside, life is taking seed. As my belly grows—as I feel life take shape in me—I am birthing myself. As a baby is conceived, so a Mother is born.

Can you hear the cracking open of my heart?

The truth is, four days after finding out that I was pregnant I gave up my story. I let it go. I surrendered, and I became HER vessel. I let myself fall in love with my baby. I let myself fall deeply, unconditionally, wildly in love. I glowed love, I oozed love in a way that I never felt possible. I finally did not care about the world "out there" or having to be someone or make anything happen. I was purely focused on what my body needed to grow this amazing miracle. I was fierce and strong and centered and at peace. I was, for the first time, at peace. I could let it all go; nothing seemed as important to me as the protection and nurturance of this sacred, holy gift. I was fully the vessel for this love to pour forth. I felt liberated. I stood looking at the flowers and the hummingbirds in my garden and let the tears of relief roll down my face.

I was in truth. I wanted to have a baby. I never knew. How could I? I moved seamlessly into Mother. I was clear. And I even loved myself through my cracking denial. I forgave myself, my mother, her mother. I stood—at last—free of the wound of being unmothered. I let it go.

Somewhere in the darkness, deep inside, life is taking seed. As my belly grows—as I feel life take shape in me—I am birthing myself. As a baby is conceived, so a Mother is born.

I am Sigune, Grief Woman—Queen of Death—holding the portal between the worlds, where loss is love and grief is liberation.

I do not want to see Her. I close my eyes tight and hope She goes away.

I do not feel well. I have been vomiting for days. I feel like I am dying. Somewhere in the recesses of my heart I know that there is something wrong. I can feel Sigune sitting on my womb. On a fated Wednesday morning, I crawl to the bathroom and vomit my entire insides out. Wretched, I curl around the toilet and weep, convulsing. I do not want anyone to see me…definitely not my darling man.

I know.

I make an excuse that I need to go to the doctor for something. I drive alone. I arrive and they show me to a room. I am dying inside; I know it.

Dr. Nona talks and I cannot hear her. All I can hear are my own screams rattling the examination room. I dare not look at the monitor. There is no heartbeat. And just like that, death grabs at me. Like the ferocious mother lion that I am, I tear back at Her. I am racked by sobs I do not know where they come from. I feel that I am dying. I am completely torn apart. I cling to Nona and she holds me.

On Oct 31, Halloween—Samhain—the day when the veils are thinnest, there is a DNC: Death…Nothing…Cease.

I am Sigune—Queen of Death—here, beloved, take my hand. We are to journey now. Come.

I collapse into Her and let Her carry me to the underworld. Days of which I have no memory pass. I am lay in Sigune's lap. I am dead. I am flailing, rageful, inconsolable. I feel like killing someone. I have lost all faith in Mother. I am destroyed.

Somewhere in this living nightmare, I stand naked in front of the mirror, shaking, sobbing. I am so alone. I am forsaken. I scream, "Why did you do this to me? Why would you give me this miracle and take it from me? Why would you be so fucking cruel?" I wonder if I am being punished because now I was suffering as my own mum had suffered. Oh, such cruelty.

I seem to be met by silence.

I was gone. No one could reach me. I did not know the way back. Have you ever had the feeling that you were done? The feeling that comes and envelops you in such despair that you cannot see the light?

There is no light.
Heart broken open
wrenched, writhed, and pried open
Nothing left to hide.
Falling into the abyss
of
clarity…
Naked nothingness, shaking free,
rattling free,
to reveal the softening of the hands that hold separate the faces of loss and gain…

PHOTOS BY HEATHER BRAND

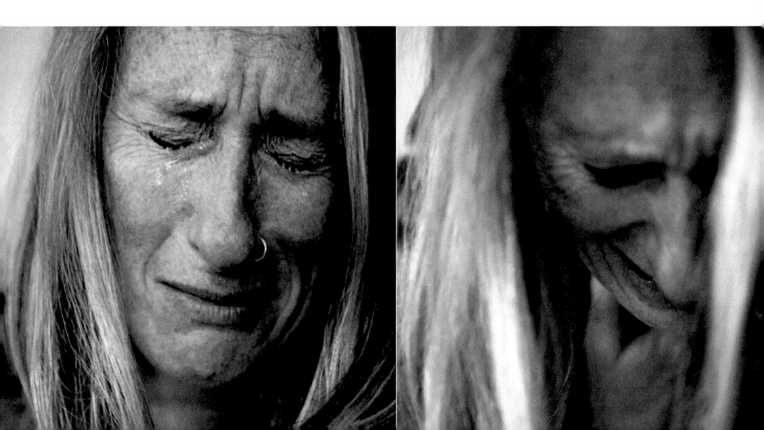

Down in the dark I lie; I have no choice. I am Inana on the meat hook, rotting away.

Who I was is dying. I am not the woman I was. I do not know if I will come back. I surrender. I let go again and again and again. I only come out to do what I have to in my world, and then I slink back into the folds of darkness. I feel Sigune's hands braiding my hair, caressing my forehead, singing a faint lullaby. I feel Her anointing my body with holy oils and weeping Her tears onto my face. I release, let go. She begins to whisper in my ear. I start to feel Her as a comfort. I nestle into Her. I hear Her whispers like a gentle breeze.

"My love, my daughter, my sweet angel. I am weaving the light and shadow of love into your heart. There are no more lies. No more places to hide. You cannot hide from life and love and loss any longer. For you have loved and lost the most precious thing that you could ever know. There is now nothing to lose. You are free…You are a vessel of love. You have received the biggest boon of all; you now know the truth of love and that you can never control it. You can only choose to live it. Risk it."

I hear Her words and let them embrace me. I write them down and read them aloud to myself. I look myself straight in the mirror and see the wisdom and humility of my own being. I see a veil of protection that I had held around myself, gone. I am raw. I am here now. I am Presence.

I feel honest, intimate with myself—and with you—in a way that I have never known before. I have been destroyed and recreated. My illusion of somehow keeping myself safe from loss, safe from experiencing the kind of loss that my own mum had experienced, is gone, washed clean in the tsunami of tears.

I am here now. I am raw now. I am present with you now.

My truth, my love, is that I would never change this story. Don't get me wrong; I would never choose this story…or at least my human self would not. My heart breaks for every woman who has felt the loss of life in her womb and could not save her baby.

I bless the golden soul that passed through the vessel of my being. This soul gave me the gift of becoming the mother that I never knew I wanted to be, that I never allowed myself to taste out of fear of loss. And now I am in deep awe of the power of being the vessel to this love, this grief, this humanity, this light, this shadow.

I welcome it all. I welcome you into me, knowing that there is only one of us here. I hold your grief and joy in my heart; they are the same thing.

AFTERWORD: Pregnancy is steeped in mystery. Today is my baby's due date. And even though I "lost" the baby, I realize, in this moment, that I have been pregnant for the last nine months. My body and soul have been in hibernation, gestating and creating. "I am birthing myself. As a baby is conceived, so a Mother is born" I wrote these words not fully "knowing" what they meant. Today I do.

Today I know that I am here to walk as Mother, to move us from our singular state of "me" to the unified state of "we." I am here to open my heart to feel the searing intimacy that this new state of consciousness truly requires of me and you. I am here to awaken that knowing within you.

I could not have told you this until now. The baby I am birthing is a new consciousness, one that leads from the preoccupation with what "I need" to the awareness of what "we need." Walking the Path of the Priestess has called me forward to be an embodied call for all of us to mother ourselves and our world, knowing in our hearts that we are one.

Through losing my baby, I lost myself; upon returning, I have found you—and the whole world—alive within my heart.

Sometimes,
I just don't know,
What I don't know,
Until…
There is a moment,
When I crack open
And in that terrifying
Liberating crack
The light of my truth
Comes flooding in.
And then
I feel
Torn tender
Vulnerable sweet honeyed agonizing pain
As the innocent eyes of my heart
are pried open,
Blinking
and
Blinded.
I am
in the stark illumination
of
What
Is
Real.

And finally I KNOW…
There is only one of us here…
And LOVE is real.

ELAYNE KALILA DOUGHTY

Elayne Kalila Doughty, MA, MFT is the Founder of **Priestess Presence—Powerful Women Changing the World** (www.Priestesspresence.com) where she offers an in depth Mystery School training for women who are called to ground in real practice, devoted embodiment, and service in the world. Elayne is passionate about opening the ancient mysteries of the Divine Feminine into our very modern-day lives so women can all step more fully into serving from a place of love, presence and purpose.

Elayne is the co-founder of **The Feminine Alchemy Immersion Program** where she offers deeply experiential and highly transformative spiritual leadership programs. Elayne also co-founded **The Global Gratitude Alliance** (www.gratitudealliance.com) which has a mission to empower and improve the lives of women, children and young adults through grassroots projects in some of the most vulnerable parts of the world. Her work at the Gratitude Alliance led her to create **The Safe Embrace Trauma Healing Program** (www.safeembracetraumahealing.org) which is the culmination of many years of work with women survivors of trauma and gender based violence. This program promotes trauma healing and empowerment for women across the globe.

As a faculty member at **The Shift Network** (www.theshiftnetwork.com), and a co-host of the **Inspiring Women Summit** (www.inspiringwomensummit.com), Elayne brings her expertise and devoted guidance to 1000's of women every year. Currently Elayne is musing her next book: *Priestess Presence – Women in Passionate Service to Healing the Heart of the World.*

Connect with Elayne at **www.ElayneDoughty.com**

Chapter 5

THE WAY OF EROTIC INNOCENCE:
AWAKEN THE PLEASURE PRIESTESS WITHIN

BY JENA LA FLAMME

I always imagined I'd grow up to be a doctor, scientist, or diplomat, so it was a great surprise to discover that my true calling was to become a priestess—specifically, a priestess of pleasure.

In my upbringing the concepts of "pleasure" and "priestess" were both absent. When it came to pleasure, the notion that self-gratification of any sort was a valid pursuit unto itself was simply unheard of. Pleasure was at best an afterthought, always measured against how much I had accomplished to earn it. An occasional reward for hard work, pleasure was something to feel guilty about, and to be careful not to have too much of. When I ate food and it tasted great, instead of relishing it, I felt anxious: afraid that I would get myself into trouble for enjoying myself too much. When I experimented with my sexuality and it felt wonderful, instead of relaxing into it, I felt guilty and ashamed.

I was a straight-A student all my life and defined my worth through my achievements. Getting good grades, performing well in music and sports, making money, and being thought of by others as either thin or cute was what I judged as valuable. The expectation that I was entitled to pleasure, and that it was indeed valuable, never even crossed my young mind.

On the contrary, I was distrustful and fearful of pleasure, and I had contempt for my body's desires. I was deeply critical of myself, including my physical form. At the tender age of twelve I remember telling myself those loaded words that ruin lives—"I'm fat." This internal dialogue began more than a decade of hating my body. I squandered my attention with a preoccupation with food and body image. I was either binge eating or restricting, but never at peace with my body's natural need to eat.

Certainly, I didn't treat my body—what I now like to call my Female Animal—as anything remotely sacred. I was raised in the Christian Church and for me God was something formless and masculine. I was taught the Earthly flesh of the female body was an inevitable source of sin, starting with so-called "Original Sin," the "crime" of being born as a result of sex. So it was no surprise that I connected my sexual nature with shame. In doing so, I was tapping into the same sexual shame that is pervasive in our culture, where we think of our bodies as lesser than our minds, and lesser than the divine, with sexuality being the least divine of all.

However, the body and the pleasures of the body were not always thought of in this way. In the big picture of humanity's evolution, it's only been in the last few thousands of years that patriarchal religions have associated the feminine as a threat to spiritual fulfillment. In this mind-centric context, the body, flesh, sensuality and nature are associated with impurity. The feminine is undervalued and blamed as a source of sin and temptation.

In contrast, the positive emphasis on the masculine in our predominant religions is striking and impossible to miss. Today our churches are mostly, if not entirely, led by men, telling stories from the Bible that are largely about men, with women portrayed as the secondary sidekicks to the main action. God is always described as a male and a father figure. The masculine is exalted and associated with holiness, purity, and transcendence over nature. The overall message is men hold the spiritual authority and that the pleasures of the body are wrong.

When I was growing up I knew that the words "priestess" and "goddess" existed, but I thought neither had contemporary relevance. I thought a priestess or a goddess were conceptual artifacts of another era, found in ancient Greek or Egyptian mythology. Yet my path has led me to discover that both concepts of pleasure and the priestess are not what I originally thought. They are extremely relevant to us as modern women, and together they hold the keys for our collective health, happiness and fulfillment.

The priestess, unlike the "priest" concept in patriarchal religion, is not a role for a select few attained by ascension through a hierarchy. If you are thinking, "Who am I to be a priestess?" the answer is, who are you not to be? All women are born as natural priestesses. As girls our bodies are full of energy, joy and wordless knowing. Guided by our innocent impulses and instincts, we are intimately connected with the world through our senses. We feel the rapture of spontaneous devotion and celebration without being taught to look for it.

Every woman has the potential to awaken the priestess archetype within her autonomously, upon her own authority. Each of us is connected to inherited universal archetypes found in world religions, myths, fairy tales, and legends, and the priestess is one of them. Any woman, no matter how unglamorous or unholy she might feel in this moment, has just as much right as any other to tap into this energy and nurture the emergence of the priestess within.

Claiming the priestess within is not about having qualities that make you superior to other women. On the contrary, she is a symbol for our interconnectedness. It doesn't require buying into any stereotype, a specific wardrobe, or appearing "spiritual." Rather than defining herself by what she knows, the priestess welcomes the mystery inherent in existence, and embraces constant discovery.

The Path of the Priestess invites you to interpret the discomforts or disappointments in your life as messengers and wakeup calls ushering you to reconnect you with something deep inside that is purely and powerfully feminine. As you connect with this source, it can feel like a deep inner reservoir of ancient wisdom that you may not have known existed. The Divine Feminine is already part of you, just waiting for you to remember and return home to her presence within you. And when you do, you become even more alive and energized. You become a greater force of light. This is a stupendous moment in your life when you decide to live from you own inner guidance, and allow the priestess archetype to divinely guide you. You feel powerful and vividly feminine, awakened and ready to shine your light.

When you are in sync with your inner priestess, you are able to get out of your own way and let your natural power flow. You know your worth and you feel empowered to create a world according to your own inner vision. You carry confidence and power which translates to influence. You can move mountains if you choose, and importantly, you know how to have a good time while doing so.

In order to fully embrace the priestess archetype, we need to free ourselves from the conditioning that teaches that our pleasure—be it sensual, sexual, spiritual or otherwise—is a sin and a source of shame. We need to reestablish the wisdom that our pleasure is innocent and pure. It is our guiding light and purpose in life. By combining these two ideals every woman can be their own pleasure priestess and live to her fullest physical, mental, emotional and spiritual expression.

While I am now willingly a pleasure priestess, espousing the innocence of pleasure and the sacredness of life as my vocation, the defining moment which set me on this path was not by my choosing. When I was 15 years old and still a virgin, I lost my innocence when I was raped on the street late at night. With a fake ID, I had gone nightclubbing with a girlfriend for the very first time. But a few hours and several drinks later, a young man I'd been dancing with brought me outside and forced himself upon me. Though I pleaded and begged him to stop, he held me down and penetrated me. I froze. I didn't even scream. Afterwards, the only way I knew to cope with this trauma was to repress the experience entirely. For years I didn't tell anyone and I tried my best to block the memory from my mind.

For the next several years I struggled with sexual boundaries with the boys and men I was consensually experimenting with. They never forced themselves past my boundaries; my problem was I never voiced them in the first place. My mind would scream "No!" but I could not get the words past my lips. I submissively offered pleasure to the bodies of my lovers, while dissociating from my own. Up until a certain point I would enjoy the sexual play, but whenever it crossed a line into feeling uncomfortable, I would freeze and didn't know how to communicate my needs. Being sexual did not feel innocent. It was wrapped in obligation, approval seeking, guilt, shame and trauma.

Then, at age 18, the pendulum began to swing the other way. I went to my first music festival and met a man named Gum who profoundly changed my life. Gum invited me to visit him in the subtropical rainforest where he lived (and still does to this day) in a solar-powered house completely made of recycled materials. His home was a lush verdant paradise among palms, ferns, and magnificent tall trees and thick vines.

A rainforest ecologist, Gum knew the land like the back of his hand and was eager to initiate me—a city girl who was scared of the wild forest—to the ways of nature. He would take me on off-trail hikes deep into the wilderness, and as he showed me how to be in harmony with the forest, my fear of nature began to fall away. To my delight, I found Mother Nature to be a kind and gentle protective force that cradled me.

I had been raised to believe that people were superior to nature, and that the trees, mountains, waters and creatures of the Earth were put here for us to conquer, subdue and use as we pleased. Yet with Gum's guidance, my arrogant sense of superiority to the Earth was humbled. I experienced how I really am one with nature. My body literally is nature. I was struck with awe at the union I felt with every creature and organism on the planet. This experience was the first crack into my conditioning that set me on the Priestess Path.

Since then, Nature has been a refuge that I turn to again and again to be replenished with wonder and vitality. Nature is the sensory-rich temple of the priestess. Long before there were

churches and cathedrals there were groves of trees, riverbanks and ocean beaches where women celebrated their connection with the divine. It is a feast for our senses—the beauty of a sunset, the tickle of a summer breeze on your skin, the theater of clouds in a blue sky. Connecting with Nature is a boundless source of pleasure. The priestess knows that we are neither greater than nor lesser than the Earth; we are inseparable.

At this stage of my journey, though I believed the Earth was sacred and that I was part of it, I still held on to my internal programming that the divine was male. Yet when I traveled to India, everything changed. I set off as a curious tourist knowing nothing about yoga, meditation or Eastern wisdom. Following the recommendation of a friend, I went to a small picturesque village in the deserts of Rajasthan called Pushkar. There I met a woman, called Misha who was visiting from California who described herself as a priestess, the first I had ever met. She took me on a walk to a temple on the top of a hill, and told me a local story of the Hindu gods and goddesses.

"This is the temple of the goddess Savitri," she told me. "She was married to Brahma and he invited her to participate in a ritual that began at a specific auspicious hour. She promised she'd be there, but when the time came she was so absorbed in what she was creating, being the goddess of creativity that she is, that she lost track of time, and did not appear at the required hour. Brahma, furious at his wife for letting him down, divorced her on the spot and married another goddess, Gayatri. Savatri, when she learned what happened, was herself enraged at Brahma and stormed off up a mountain. Gayatri, when she realized the full context of her sudden marriage with Brahma, was also furious and stormed up another mountain. This hill we are standing on is where Savitri went which is why this is her temple. And that hill," Misha said pointing to another hill nearby protruding from the desert, "this is where Gayatri went, and that is her temple."

As she told the story that was intimately connected to the geography in which we were situated, I realized that the experiences of the Hindu deities describe an existence much like the dramas of humanity. I began to see how the gods and goddesses are metaphors for our own divine nature. We are the gods and goddesses, even in our present, imperfect state.

This was a complete flip in my consciousness. I had been raised to think that God the Father in Heaven and Jesus his Son were the divine, and that humans were not. Now I was being confronted with a life-changing question: What if all of it is divine? What if I am not separate from the divine right now, as I am? What if the divine is experiencing itself through me?

In that moment I fully embraced the concept of the Divine Feminine, the Goddess that up until that moment had been entirely missing from my spiritual life. I sensed her as a crystal chandelier with a million faces, each of them a woman with her own unique expression of a greater light, the feminine force that unites us all. I felt immediately connected to every woman on the planet and implicitly accepted that we are all sisters. I understood right then that I am a goddess as well. All women are.

Eventually I concluded that to be a priestess is to be an advocate and ambassador for the Divine Feminine. The Divine Feminine is a presence, an experience, and a knowing born deep inside. The Goddess is someone you can see in yourself—you can experience yourself as a contemporary female deity. The sacred feminine is understandable on a mental level, but even if a priestess has never read a book on the topic, she feels it in her soul. The Goddess is more than a mental concept or a figure from an ancient past. She is a felt experience that teaches us that we are not small, insignificant creatures down below an all-knowing God on high. We are each threads inextricably woven into the complete tapestry of the divine.

The spiritual teachings I discovered in India also challenged the way I valued myself. I learned that if you pin your happiness on an external object, person or achievement, there is always a risk of it disappearing, and with it your happiness vanishing too. You may think having the dream job, man, body, car, house or lifestyle will fulfill you, but none of these things are guaranteed to last, and deluding yourself that they will is a sure path to misery. True happiness and satisfaction arises from within and is something you don't even have to create. It's already there. You just need to learn to be present with your true nature that is peace and happiness itself.

I realized how much I was looking outside of myself for external validation and satisfaction and I began to turn my focus inward. I started meditating regularly, and as I contacted stillness within, beneath the babble of my judging, labeling mind, I felt my whole personality transform for the better. I felt more grounded, less needy of external approval. I felt physically stronger and therefore more protected. Through the yogic practices of meditation, asanas (postures) and pranayama (breathwork) I learned to calm my nervous system and stay in the present. I learned that I could experience my feelings no matter how uncomfortable they could be. I became less reactive and more able to respond with flexibility. I could listen to my inner thoughts and know what was right for me without needing to look outside of myself for signs of approval. It felt like liberation.

Soon after, my journey along the Priestess Path took another important turn when I stumbled upon a book about Earth-based religion by Starhawk, who spelled out on the pages in black and white, "All pleasure, harm it none, is in honor of the Goddess."

The idea of pleasure being in service of the divine sent a shock through my system, yet the words instantly resonated as true. I began to understand that pleasure is not shameful, not even neutral; it is sacred. The reason pleasure is sacred is because it connects our awareness to the pulse of life through the senses. The mentality of sacred pleasure is "What better way to honor the sacred than by thoroughly enjoying our existence?"

Consciously experienced pleasure reminds us of that divinity is here and now, in the moment, on Earth, and contingent upon where we put our attention.

When I encountered these teachings I instantly felt layers of shame, especially about food and sex, melt away. I saw that the beautiful sensual and sexual experiences that I had authentically enjoyed yet felt ashamed of really did not hurt anyone, including myself. I became more comfortable with my sexual nature, and granted myself the freedom to unabashedly enjoy every aspect of it.

The idea of "all pleasure, harm it none" makes the critical distinction between what I now call true pleasure and counterfeit pleasure. Counterfeit pleasure is the type that feels compulsive and makes you feel worse after having it, like the hangover after too much alcohol or the sugar coma after an ice cream binge. However, the sacred pleasure I'm advocating for is something completely different. True pleasure feels good while you are experiencing it, and in the aftermath. It feels like a choice—it is one opportunity to feel good among many. And it is sustainable, meaning that enjoying it makes you feel better, which in turn allows you to enjoy more of it in the future.

A pleasure priestess is aware of this difference, and makes of a practice of discerning between the two. She knows that true pleasures are a conscious choice, and that the best ones are virtually free. When we embrace the values of pleasure, we relish in the fact that it is available to everyone. This democratic nature of pleasure means that the more people are enjoying themselves, the more pleasurable it is. This principle can help you create a lifestyle that is nourishing and pleasurable for all.

Being present is a skill that many spiritual traditions encourage and that is a requirement for true pleasure to occur. True pleasure only exists in the present, and unless you are present, you are not experiencing pleasure at all. In evolutionary terms, once upon a time there was no choice but to live completely in the present—that's all our brain power could handle. But as we developed the advanced centers of our brain that grant us the perception of the passing of time, we were given the ability to place our attention on the past or to think about the future. And while there's nothing wrong with reminiscing about the past or dreaming about the future, being engaged in the present moment is the principle point of life.

You can think of true pleasure as meditation in disguise. Whereas the practice of meditation may focus your mind on your breath, or a mantra or creative visualization, the practice of pleasure requires that you are completely aware of what you are experiencing through the senses. Being fully present means being present to mind, emotions, and body at the same time, and is the secret to a liberated, pleasure-filled existence. True pleasure does not have to feel like something is happening, but it does feel like nothing is missing. As I continued to practice yoga and meditation and became more present and aware, the repressed memory of my rape came over me like a tidal wave of such intensity that I could no longer ignore what had happened. For the first time, I allowed myself to feel my anger towards the rapist. Giving myself space to heal, I retreated once again to Gum's rainforest and faced the agony of my lost innocence, and the injustice of someone else's sexuality being forced upon me. I sat with my pain, rage, and anguish. I screamed and cried an ocean of tears.

It was a healing process that took time and as I made it through, I embraced one of the most powerful tools for healing shame: transparency. I began to tell my story. In the telling, and in the presence of my friends and their compassionate listening, I felt the wound of this violation begin to heal. This was something that happened to me that was not my fault. Instead of being ashamed of my experience I could be proud of the fact that I was honestly facing what happened and healing my wounds.

I have come to understand that the world is not always safe place. Things happen that we don't want to happen, and they aren't our fault, but ultimately we can heal and rise above our traumas. I also learned that if I am going to be safe I have to be aware and present, and take responsibility for setting boundaries and protecting myself. Even though my innocence had been stolen, I could reclaim it.

This process of reclamation and healing has led me to the discovery of erotic innocence, a term coined by author Saida Désilets, that beautifully puts words to something I had come to feel instinctively deep in my bones. As my understanding of the divine expanded to include

a goddess who smiled joyfully on my sexuality and gave her blessing to pleasure, I started to treat sex as a sacred act. Sex, once entwined with negativity, became a treasured expression of my spirituality. It became my celebration and prayer. I explored the feelings and sensations in my body and recognized that my authentic pleasure—not the dissociated pleasure intended to please another, but my own true pleasure—was always innocent and pure.

The Greek root of the word erotic is eros meaning, "that which animates life." Saida Desilets describes erotic innocence as the undomesticated, unconditioned response of your body to anything in life that triggers aliveness and therefore pleasure. If we understand erotic in this context then it is impossible to segregate it to any one area of the body or mind, as eros imbues everything: it's inherent in every part of the matrix of life.

Your erotic innocence is your body's innate impulse towards all that gives you delight. Your instinctual drive towards feeling good is fundamentally innocent because this impulse is rooted in your pre-lingual, pre-cognitive, sensing, reptilian brain, the part which developed earliest, long before the thinking, judging mind existed. It is neither right or wrong, it just is.

Imagine how sexually freeing it would be to have all your mind's judgments quieted so you could directly hear your body's yearnings? While it can feel humbling and even frightening for the mind to step down from its vigilant role, even for a moment, the rewards for doing so are rich and exciting. When you can suspend judgment over your body's desires, and hold back from labeling your desires as good or bad, allowed or forbidden, then you are in touch with your erotic innocence.

Recognizing the innocence of your desire invites more pleasure into your life, including in your sensuality and sexuality. You have the capacity to enjoy immense sexual satisfaction, including multiple and varied forms of orgasms. When you remove the shame and grant yourself complete sexual freedom, every fantasy that you can envision becomes a possibility.

There's an unspoken belief in our society that a good wife and mother should be willing to sacrifice her own sexual and creative needs for her family's sake. A pleasure priestess rejects this concept and claims her right to a creative, unbridled sex life. She owns her innate sexiness at any age, shape, or size. The media stereotypes that reduce being sexy to the extremes of a porn star or an androgynous teenage girl are pervasive, but they are only a small representation of what being sexy fully encompasses. If you judge your own sexiness by those standards, you will be cutting yourself off from your erotic innocence. But when you define your sexiness in your own terms, your erotic innocence is unleashed.

My definition of being sexy is being united with your primal sexual self, exuding it, and enjoying it. It is not conforming to what magazines tell you being sexy is supposed to look like. It doesn't carry inauthentic undertones; in fact it is the authentic expression of who you are. Even if you think your ass is too fat, your belly is too round, your breasts are too small or your thighs too big, when you are in touch with your erotic innocence— the sexual pulse that animates you and animates all life—you are sexy.

Erotic innocence is not just about sex; it is about making a conscious choice to pay attention to whatever opens and enlivens you. When you are in touch with your erotic innocence you walk through life with your senses heightened. You experience pleasure everywhere you go. You become acutely in touch with what feels good and what doesn't. When you are connected with your erotic innocence, the notion that "you don't know what you want" evaporates, as you are always able to know your preferred choice in a given moment. When you allow your erotic innocence to guide you in the world, your experience transforms, as you are continuously led from one small delight in life to another. Whether you are aroused by the curve of a tree while walking in a forest and stimulated to creative heights in your career, for your erotic innocence, being turned on is a synonym for being alive.

In order to experience erotic innocence, you must cultivate the capacity to say no. As I mentioned, I used to be terrible at saying no when it came to sexual advances, but I'm proud to say that over time I have become a master of healthy boundaries. Now I am easily attuned to what my body needs to feel comfortable and safe and I am at ease communicating my needs clearly to others.

I am no longer stressed out by the idea of upholding sexual boundaries as needed, and this has allowed me to feel sexy, receptive, and safe all at the same time. As a pleasure priestess I am a free spirit—I have sex the way I want it. I know that I can exude my natural, unstifled sensuality while having impeccable boundaries and that these two are compatible. One of the main reasons women tone down their innate pleasure priestess energy is because of the sexual attention that often immediately comes with it. But when you become more confident with setting boundaries, verbally and with body language, you too will experience being sexy as being safe. A pleasure priestess can effortlessly say no and deflect unwanted attention using phrases like, "That's not a match for me," "I don't feel like it," "I need some privacy and alone time."

When you are connected with the guiltless, shameless nature of your erotic innocence, you are fully embracing the Priestess Path. You don't feel the need to rush frantically through life seeking one pleasure hit after another. Rather you can breathe deeply and go absolutely nowhere if you please because you know that pleasure is always there for you.

The Priestess Path is a path of sovereignty. A priestess is aware of how our culture has wounded, devalued, and limited the feminine, robbing it of its inherent sacredness, and the sexism of spirituality that depicts the divine as exclusively male, yet she refuses to live in a victim role; she knows herself as a creatrix.

A fully awakened priestess does not look outside of herself for confirmation that she is valuable. The opinions of others do not have a binding spell over her. She does not stifle her truth or pander to others' approval, and her self-assured attitude is magnetic. She knows her magical nature and she knows her worth. She engages in life in her own unique way. And when she does, she becomes a legend of her own time. Her presence is electric because she is not looking to you for proof that she is attractive. She knows it. She feels it. She also releases herself from the expectations of self-sacrifice and over-nurturing or over-managing others and their expectations. She is confident in her autonomy.

Patriarchal religion does not give us spiritual role models that we can relate to, so the priestess steps up to become a role model herself. Priestesses retrieve forgotten stories and are the cutting-edge story-tellers of their own. We were taught that men go on quests and create history, while women stay behind, waiting for them. No longer! The Priestess Path is its own quest. We are both the main characters and authors of our own mythologies. We are creating history.

The pleasure priestess is not quiet about what she believes. She loves herself and the fact that she is female. She values her inner wisdom including listening, intuition, nurturing, and creativity. She cultivates her sexuality and recognizes that it is a learned art. She is open to exploring her deepest passions and what moves her profoundly. Whether she is single or has a partner, or multiple, she requires sensual and sexual pleasure in her life and makes it a priority.

You may have been raised to believe that pleasure and sex were antithetical to spirituality. But imagine how differently you would perceive yourself and your sexuality if you had been mentored by a pleasure priestess and had learned at an early age that it was sacred. If you've felt in the past that you had to make that choice, I want to reassure you that you can deeply enjoy your body's pleasure-seeking, sexual nature and still be a spiritual woman. In fact, the two go hand in hand as the essence of feminist spirituality.

As a priestess you can experience that everything that is alive is an interconnected part of the same web of life. While it's possible to attain this experience through chanting, fasting, praying or meditating, for many women, accessing divine union with existence is most accessible through sex, including self-pleasuring. The classic phrase we cry out in the throes of climax—"Oh my God!"—sums it up perfectly. In truly good sex you have the experience of being one with all of life. This is why the experience of pleasure and ecstasy are inherently sacred. When we get to be in expanded states of pleasure in which we don't know where we end and the universe begins, we are having a direct experience of the divine.

The prevalent myth about pleasure is that it is frivolous and shallow, but in actual fact, pleasure leads us to understand the deepest significance of our existence. At some point, everyone asks themselves the question, "What is the meaning of Life?" My answer is pleasure. Having pleasure in life and having meaning in life is one and the same. Pleasure teaches that life itself wants to be savored, relished, and appreciated. Whenever I ask someone what gives their life meaning and why, their final response always boils down to, "It makes me feel good," indicating that whatever brings them pleasure gives their life meaning. I invite you to embrace the Priestess Path: recognize the sacredness of your female body as an emanation of the feminine divine, and infuse your life with the blessings of pleasure.

About the Author

JENA LA FLAMME

Jena la Flamme is a weight loss expert, author of *Pleasurable Weight Loss: The Secrets of Feeling Great, Losing Weight and Loving Your Life Today,* and the founder of the Pleasurable Weight Loss movement. Her profound teachings show that contrary to popular belief, pleasurable weight loss is not a contradiction in terms.

During her ten-year struggle with food, weight, and bad body image, Jena despised her body and was highly suspicious of pleasure. This lasted until she discovered that her issue wasn't that she was having too much pleasure, it was that she wasn't having enough! As she learned to trust the wisdom of her female body and to trust pleasure, she came to peace with food and her body transformed. She now shows women how to do the same through her blog, online programs, live Pleasure Camps, social media, and private coaching.

She has been featured in *Elle, Glamour,* and *Prevention* magazine. For more information, visit her website at **www.jenalaflamme.com** or get her free "7 Days of Pleasurable Weight Loss" e-program at **www.pleasurableweightloss.com.**

BURN THE IVORY TOWER
(MAKING IT SAFE TO BE POWERFUL)

BY JENNIFER RUSSELL

We, as women, have been taught we need to reign our energy in.

We've been taught that our chaotic emotional beauty is a little too much to handle for the world. It's not linear and goal oriented. It's not predictable and controllable. Unbridled, you are too messy and too much. Femininity should be subtle, alluring, even feint. So let's rein it in and be good little girls. Let's get our good grades. Let's get married young. Let's be the property of our fathers and then our husbands. Let's be defined by our children and *their* accomplishments. Even dressed up in post-feminism, gender-equality, and goddess-wear, we still act as if it is *unsafe to be fully our feminine selves.* That's been the unfortunate modern story of the feminine, *until now.*

We all have the archetype of the *goody-two-shoes* living in us. The good girl. The dutiful daughter. The high achiever that wants to excel, fit *inside* the existing system—win awards and be recognized—but not to draw too far outside the lines.

We all have the archetype of the *holly homemaker* whose duty is the happy life of family and husband, whose impact is limited to the people within the household and whose contribution is taken for granted and virtually invisible outside of the home.

And we all have some of the shadow archetypes, too. The bitch: a woman that is too assertive. The slut: a woman who expresses her sexuality too much, and is able to get what she wants. The witch: a woman who possesses unexplainable powers and questionable motives. (It's worth noting that the masculine forms of these archetypes are lauded. Bitchiness in a man is considered confidence. A male slut is crowned "Don Juan". A male witch is simply a magician.)

Where are the positive archetypes of feminine power? Kali, who cuts off your head? Hera, who is the god form of *holly homemaker*: basically "Zeus' wife" with a goddess-sized jealous streak? Wonder Woman, who battles evil but has no family and no love in her life? It's time for us to tell a new story of femininity, with our choices, with our self-expression, and with our lives. There are too few positive examples of women who are in full command of their sexuality and its attractive powers. There are too few healthy stories of women who's full creative expression is unbridled and uncontrolled.

It's no wonder women hold back their power. We've made being powerful very *unsafe*. To be powerful in the face of thousands of years of patriarchical expectations is to go against all of your social contracts and upbringing—to risk being a pariah that is bitchy and slutty and home-wrecking and out of place. Its no wonder that we live in a culture of women that don't take leadership roles, don't promote themselves effectively, that aren't enough of the influencers and future-shapers that get written about in our history books. There are a few exceptions, of course. Because of the courage of feminists and activists like Susan B. Anthony, Nobel Peace Prize winner Jane Addams, Maya Angelou, Lucille Ball, and Gloria Steinem, the 21st century welcomes the feminine (instead of outright suppressing and repressing her). But feminine *power* is still not recognized for its role in shaping our world. The power to shape events flows naturally through you. Your biology is honed and optimized to wield it. It is your birthright.

On the day of my high school graduation, I stood at the podium receiving just about every type of award they could hand out. Math, language, science, grades, physical fitness, talent shows; my inner *goody-two-shoes* and future *holly homemaker* couldn't have been more proud. But even though I was walking through life playing all these roles, another part of me was starting to question whether playing these roles was actually going to lead to the happy life it was supposed to. I wasn't seeing a lot of evidence that the people making up the rules to the game understood how to win it. There was a part of me that knew I couldn't fit all of myself into these archetypes, and that part of me grew restless being unexpressed.

Over time that part of me became *the woman screaming inside me.* Mostly, I kept her quiet, until the day I couldn't any longer.

In college, there was a boy—6'2", blonde, blue eyes, charming, and sexy. He'd been a male model, and every girl within a ten-mile radius had a crush. He had a perfect body, he was smart, he was funny, and he was my boyfriend. He was also misogynist, jealous, and angry. I wasn't happy, but my cultural training as a woman was telling me I should be. One afternoon I caught a glimpse of myself walking with him in a reflection. The *screaming woman inside me* saw it, too. Neither of us liked what we saw.

I was walking behind him—always behind, never beside—eyes downcast because he didn't want me to look at anyone else. It would have been a stretch to call our relationship abusive, but it was certainly destructive. The woman in the reflection was unhappy, small, diminished. I didn't like her.

"I'm sure that you, like so many other women, want to marry him," his brother said to me later that day. Something in me snapped lose.

"Actually no, I don't" said the *screaming woman inside me* in a calm, measured voice.

I broke up with him and swung the pendulum the other way as far as I could. If I was the epitome of the traditional feminine—soft, sensitive, and content to be in the background—I rejected and made wrong those parts of me, becoming fiercely independent, strong minded, under no-one's thumb. I leapt to the other half of the schism. I wanted my power back.

I entered the biotech workforce by storm, thinking that emotions were best left at home, feelings were irrelevant, and that nothing was to be taken personally in business. I took on a mountain of work and plowed through it, sometimes collaborating with others but more often letting them know that their work was just too inferior.

I was working in my dream job, and giving everything to it. From the age of 5, I've yearned to leave the planet better than I found it, and this biotech company was using science to do just that—ridding the world of toxins in our air, pesticides, and food.

It was because I loved the work so much that it broke my heart to hear the Senior VP that hired me say, "You've had an incredible impact on this company. I want to give you a raise and give you more responsibility. We love you, but your peers don't. They respect you, but they don't want to work with you because you are just too hard."

My heart sank as I realized the truth of what he was saying. I had become aggressive and masculine. Part of having more influence includes learning how to bring out the best in other people, not just having high expectations of them. I was on the team of getting the *job* done, but I wasn't on the *human* team.

Humbled again, I knew I needed to learn how to reintegrate my own feminine. To embrace more feminine ideals like collaboration, cooperation, sensitivity, inspiration, and empowerment, but without diminishing myself or my voice. To have the impact I wanted to have, I needed to access all of myself and find my power in flexibility and range. Not by shutting down the feminine and not demonizing the masculine, but utilizing both to be the fullest expression of myself. To make being powerful safe by bringing beauty as well as strength, finesse as well as force, and compassion as well as passion.

The Unworkable Balancing Act

I realized I was leaving at least half my power on the table; I didn't need to work on being *less* of anything. I needed to become more of *everything*. When you're not all the way right with being powerful you end up living life with a thousand little "pull-backs", always trying to be less of yourself in each situation. It makes logical sense to avoid negative ways of being. You don't want to be too meek AND you also don't want to 'make too much of yourself'. You don't want to be "too forceful" AND you don't want to be "too weak", so every time you feel yourself getting close to either one, you pull back. You pull back from being too quiet, and pull back from being too loud. What happens when you are trying to balance between these two negatively opposite poles? Your behavior becomes a thousand subtle compromises. I was seeing it in myself, and seeing from women everywhere.

From this vantage, you are never actually free to just go *all the way* in any direction. You end up living life as an unworkable balancing act, suspended between two negatives that you want to avoid. And power can never come from making less of yourself until you narrowly fit inside the box marked '100% approved'. It can't come from pulling back. It can only come from expanding into yourself fully.

Most of us have it that being powerful isn't safe. The idea, "power corrupts" is somewhere in our mind and the image we see is someone seeking power for it's own sake, and what's more it's often at the expense or detriment of another. This version of power is one we are right to be wary of. But it's time to reclaim the word "power" in our new cultural lexicon and give it a makeover. It's not the dirty word we were once taught it was. As women especially, it is absolutely needed for us to embrace rather than reject the idea of power in our lives in order to claim our true birthright.

What if you could adopt a definition of power that was pure? Incorruptible? A definition of power that you knew you never needed to pull back from. To do that, you would have to let go of the unhealthy stories you tell yourself about power. You would have to learn that ideas like *selfishness, manipulation, and greed* are what corrupts...not power. You would have to trust your own feminine to nurture those around you. You would have to realize that your positive intentions grow stronger when you are more powerful, not weaker.

Incorruptible power is based on your most *transcendent* values—values that are good for everyone when multiplied by infinity across every person, across all cultures, and across time. Values like compassion, freedom, and devotion, and love are transcendent values. They can't be corrupted because "more" for one means more for everyone.

With this understanding, the nature of power converts from a delicate balance to a transcendent value, from something corruptible to something trustable, from something that leads our culture off track toward a compass for your actions, allowing you to be more free than you have ever been to follow your impulses to their limits. To learn how to wield power that is truly in service to transcendent values, you will have to tell yourself a new story about power. So, what is that new, healthy story?

Masculine   Feminine

Active

Passive

I searched for the sources of my power. I looked within and without. I studied martial arts, public speaking, classical piano, science, and leadership. I looked at the brightest corners of my passion and purpose and the darkest corners of BDSM and sexuality. What I found is that power is sourced in polarities. Polarity is the state of having two opposite tendencies or aspects, but far from opposing each other they are actually complementary, interconnected, and interdependent, and each gives rise to the other. Like electrical power needs a "+" and a "-", our power is made up of equal and opposite energies that work in harmony with each other to motivate, inspire, direct, and attract change.

We think of power as an assertive energy; a willingness to penetrate the space and change it. We think of power as the force that people use to assert their own way, their own values, or their own aesthetic. The picture of power in our heads is usually a very active, masculine picture—like a man at the podium giving a powerful speech or a warrior leading a charge into battle. But it turns out that this *active masculine* power is just one of four faces of a whole system that makes up the complete picture of human influence.

It turns out that there is an *active* and *passive* form of masculine power and there is an *active* and *passive* form of feminine power. Together, they form the four faces of incorruptible power that combine to give you a more complete story of what it means to be powerful.

If you feel, like I did at first, that some of these faces of power are more "you" and some are not, search carefully inside yourself for little whispers of how you could explore more of the ways that feel least familiar. It's not about being something that you're not. It's about finding the parts of you that are *already powerful* and letting them out to play. If you feel unwilling to play with any one of these faces, it is likely to be the one that you most need to champion.

The Active Masculine—
Penetration

The Active Masculine – Penetration

Embodying your active masculine means noticing when something is out of alignment for you and being courageous enough to change it with purpose and urgency. The active masculine is the willingness to assert your aesthetic into the space. To *penetrate* the space with your aesthetic. Your "aesthetic" is your set of values or ideals of what should or shouldn't be. How people should or shouldn't act. It is your take on how the environment should or shouldn't feel.

To get in touch with the active masculine you are getting in touch with your judgments and complaints. We've learned to have a negative relationship to our judgments—to judge our judgments and to judge ourselves for having judgments. Everybody knows it's better not to judge people. We aspire towards acceptance of others by making our judgments wrong and wishing we didn't have them. Instead of just throwing them away and thinking you shouldn't have judgments, realize that underneath each one is the possibility and the vision of a better way.

Your judgments are a vital key to your vision for the world around you. In order to conjure a judgment you have to be able to contrast what's occurring with your unarticulated idea of what it should be instead. When those two things are in conflict your emotional distress around that is your judgment. That means your vision for the world is much more detailed and specific than you likely imagined it could be. It also means that the judgments that upset you the most are correlated to the violations to your aesthetic that you care about the most. Your judgments give you a map to what you'd like to be different and a sense of your priorities for which changes are most urgent.

To embody the active masculine, you have to trust that if you want something to change it's actually a service to you and to everyone else. What we really find unsavory about judgmental people is that they are disengaged from causing it to be different. When you combine a judgment with engagement, you get power—not complaint. Take responsibility for penetrating the space to make the world into the one you imagine, and you will inspire people to follow and help you do the same.

To invoke the active masculine, know what you value and penetrate the space until your values are pervasive. If you value compassion, the active masculine intervenes everywhere it sees a lack of compassion and inserts that. If you value cooperation, the active masculine intervenes to create the common purpose inspiring them to commit to the collective objective. If you value passion and romance, the active masculine intervenes to inject a spark and challenge your partner to rise to the occasion.

The Passive Masculine—
Holding Space

The Passive Masculine – Holding Space

To embody the passive masculine, first let go of your need to assert. Instead of penetrating the space, the passive masculine is willing to step back and hold space for all those around him. The passive masculine inspires others to express themselves by being willing to fully receive them. It's full presence and unconditional attention, an opening for another person's expression without any agenda about what that expression should be. It is powerful because it can bring out in others what otherwise would always choose to remain silent.

It is facing the void. It is standing at the doorway of possibility and allowing it to stay open without filling it. It's about creating a strong and safe container for others to express themselves. The passive masculine is able to give space for any opinions, including those that are in opposition to him.

Imagine a leader who can't hold space for other people to inject their thoughts, their creativity, their ideas, or their feelings into the discussion. Imagine a leader that could only assert. Imagine how hard it would be to follow that leader.

Imagine a romantic partner that couldn't just "be" in the presence of your emotions. That won't let you finish your sentence without adding their opinion of what you should do or how you should act. Imagine how hard it would be to express the deepest parts of you.

These leaders and lovers need to develop their passive masculine, letting go of the need to assert and leaving room for the fertile void—the space that contains nothing and therefore makes everything possible.

If leaving space for other people is difficult then the passive masculine is the one to develop. If when conflict or opposition arises you impulsively want to run away, hide it, fade it or fix it, then you need to develop your passive masculine. Show up fully and bring your full attention to another person, but without an agenda of how they should react. This requires a strong masculine, but is completely passive. If someone has ever *held space* for you, you will recognize the natural response, which is spontaneous authentic expression. This expression is the exact opposite of holding space, which is the essence of the *active feminine*.

The Active Feminine – Creative Expression

Traditionally people see the feminine as passive, demure, quiet, nurturing and kind. This is one flavor of the feminine but there is a more active feminine form which is exuberant, loud, explosive, and bright. It is the intuitive, spontaneous, power, and beauty of creative expression. The *active feminine* power is creativity herself.

If the active masculine relies on discriminative intelligence to analyze, compare, and use past experience to plan the future, the active feminine uses intuitive intelligence which picks up infinite multiple inputs simultaneously from the entire room and everyone in it—otherwise known as *the field*—and responds spontaneously moment by moment to fill the space with what's most needed.

This intuitive intelligence can let go of the 'plan' and respond spontaneously to what the moment requires. It's the ability to tap into and fill the space with exactly what's needed even before your mind knows completely what you are saying and doing.

To be in touch with the active feminine you are in touch with the field and feel what it needs—a field you and everyone in proximity to you is a part of. That often requires pausing long enough to hear the subtle impulses that tells you what's needed. Much like a musician improves a song, the active feminine feels into what's called for in the moment, following her intuitive impulses.

To embody this form of power, let go of the plan. Address what's happening now. If you are stuck with the plan and you fail to plug in to what's actually happening you are not flexible enough to be a powerful leader. Develop finesse to tell the difference between what you need and what the field is calling for moment to moment. It requires you to be fully present as your active feminine can't be preplanned, strategized or rehearsed.

Once in touch with the needs of the field, you have to do something really courageous. You must feel the whisper of your impulses and reply with a resounding, "Yes!" Don't just *say*, "Yes!" but *be* a "Yes!"

To fully be a "Yes!" to your impulses as you are feeling the field, you have to trust your intuition. If you pause long enough to evaluate whether it was a good idea the field has already moved on, the moment has passed, and you didn't express your active feminine. With connection to the field on the one hand and being a full yes to the impulses that arise with that connection on the other, you become intuition itself, which is one of the defining characteristics of the high priestess.

The high priestess is creative, she trusts her intuition, and she has the maturity and wisdom to know the difference between her egoic needs and what's truly needed in the space. Sometimes it's best for her to express what's needed herself. Sometimes it is more powerful if it would come from others. So how can she *powerfully attract* what's needed if her intuition tells her it should come from elsewhere?

The Passive Feminine – Attraction / Seduction

The *passive feminine* is the very force of attraction or magnetism. It's the ability to inspire those around you to want to come near and *seduce* them to join your cause, bringing out the best in them. Helen of Troy was the "face that launched one thousand ships" demonstrating just how powerful the passive feminine can be. It's the principle of magnetism (not just sexual attraction) and like gravity, its power to attract is irresistible.

I use the metaphor of *seduction* for this polarity to highlight the difference between the active masculine which pushes or penetrates into the space while the passive feminine literally creates more of a gravitational pull towards her in the space—much like a woman seducing a man with a twinkle in her eye; he can't help but look and is inspired to come near.

Instead of seeking power herself, the passive feminine seeks to empower those around her. Compelling leaders who understand the passive feminine polarity of attraction understand how to magnetize people to their cause. Interacting with this kind of leader allows you to witness a wave of massive support, alignment amongst peers, people passionately devoted to the mission or larger purpose of the project. Like a black hole—the most powerful attractive force in the known universe—the source of attraction is often invisible. All that can be seen is the flurry of activity around her, busy manifesting her vision.

To develop the passive feminine you must learn to set the stage for others to contribute. It is similar to *holding space* in that others are inspired and active, but different because *attraction* also includes a clear point on the horizon towards which everyone is drawn toward. The passive feminine holds the context while those around her create the content—the actions, the resources, and the effort of the interaction.

As you explore the *four faces of power,* you will likely find, as I did, that some of these forms of power are more familiar, more safe to express than others for you. Some forms may feel foreign,

risky, or even dangerous. As I describe them, feel these four faces of power within you, and take off of automatic your way of relating to them. If you find yourself judging or pulling back, take another look and see what's behind that. Only once you recognize and even love these forces within you can you truly have the influence you were meant to have.

To be the woman—or human for that matter—who has at her beck and call the ability to express her power fully, backed by a commitment to transcendent values, become intimate with each of these four faces of power. One of the highest leverage things we can do when one of these faces is out of balance is to champion the other thus gaining the range of both.

Learn to feel into each moment and know exactly the time and place for each. Strive to be equally comfortable in your masculine or feminine, using your discriminative intelligence to penetrate the space or your intuitive intelligence to throw away the plan and let creativity blossom. Learn to be comfortable with no agenda, holding space with your passive masculine ability to allow those around to swell with emotions without taking them own as your own. And cultivate your seductive femininity, letting the subtlest indication of your desires inspire a flurry of activity around you. If you want to be as powerful as you were designed to be, your work lies in developing the behavioral flexibility and range to be equally comfortable in any role rather than identifying as one.

Burn The Ivory Tower

I sometimes think we've built an ivory tower for ourselves. Where the feminine feels safe to the world, and where it feels safe to us. From the tower we can look out at the world and be inspired by what is beautiful and outraged by what is not. We can join women's circles and post pictures of sunsets on our social media vision boards. Where we can be beautiful and think pretty thoughts, but where we have no direct contact with the world we want to change. Some of us may be waiting until we feel strong enough or brave enough to leave the tower and venture out onto the Earth, taking a stand for what we believe in and leading those around us to a better future. But strength and courage can't be found in the tower. They arise only when our feet touch the Earth, we interact directly with the world in need, and we practice being the most powerful beings we can be.

There's so much to do—because we can, and because we must. But I don't want to do it alone. When I see someone who has the capability to have a positive impact in the world I really want to play with them and what's more, I really want them to play with me.

We all have a sacred obligation to impact the world in a positive way. I've felt it all my life. Don't sit back and let another breath go by without doing the good in the world that you know you are here to do. We are all here to do our good work—our best work.

To do that, you must become comfortable with a lot more discomfort than most people. You have to be willing to feel the world. I'm brought to tears both by the profound beauty in the world and the profound pain in the world. I'm inspired by humanity's creativity and heartbroken by its insolence. There's intense tragedy to feel and there's great awe and reverence. Your willingness to feel all of it—the full intensity of it—and to get nearer to that intensity is what will fuel your strength and courage.

I implore you, fulfill your sacred obligation and fulfill on the possibility of who you can become when you are your most powerful. Leave every room you enter permanently changed, marked by your beliefs and aesthetic. Let every room you enter change you, opening your channel wider to self-expression. Integrate your masculine and feminine, and make this declaration of your own power:

"I will offer what is missing.
Not what I think is most "like me".
I will offer that which balances.
Not that which mirrors or matches the group.
I will offer what is most needed.
Not what is most expected."

About the Author

JENNIFER RUSSELL

Jennifer Russell is a dyed-in-the-wool entrepreneur, having worked exclusively in high impact start-ups, most recently as president of an environmental chemical company, bringing more than 40 new technology products to market. Her dedication to the intersection of creativity and productivity has made her famous for "getting more done by accident than most people get done on purpose."

Whether it is guiding a cancer drug through the arduous process of testing and development or guiding an entrepreneur through the harrowing process of creating their business, Jennifer's insight and inspiration are bar none.

Jennifer has helped thousands of entrepreneurs create 6-, 7-, and 8-figure mission-driven businesses with a unique combination of business strategy and deeply transformative identity level work. These programs incorporate the best of NLP, the human potential movement, family systems, collaborative systems, neuroscience, and sacred theater.

In the spring of 2014, she joined Critical Path Global, a non-profit organization dedicated to creating an omni-considerate and well informed global population that understands the magnitude and urgency of our world's problems and brings together the brightest global strategists, futurists, data scientists, systems thinkers, researchers, world leaders and technologists to help create a new roadmap for humanity. Critical Path's is developing a Planetary Operating System that provides us with the shortest path to a fundamentally redesigned world-system that makes possible and supports the highest quality of life for all life and helps fundamentally alleviate poverty, war, carbon emissions, species extinction, etc.

Learn More: **www.jennifersrussell.com**

Jessica
Cornejo Gallegos

ANCIENT WISDOM FROM THE HEART

BY JESSICA CORNEJO GALLEGOS

The Inca High Priestess within me today was always inside of me. I just didn't know her. I didn't even know myself.

My family is from the Southern Andean region of Peru. My parents, my younger brother, and I lived with my grandmother in her home. She was my mother's adoptive mother and the only grandmother I really got to know.

Growing up in Lima, the capital city of Peru, I would have never imagined that so much struggle and endless days of deep darkness would be ahead for me. As a child in a traditional family, I felt nurtured and secure, perhaps even overly protected. My family was very affectionate, and I had a tight bond with my parents. My mother was my best friend, and I shared everything with her—probably much more than many children would. Money was tight, but my parents and my grandmother found ways to treat me and my younger brother. I must admit, I was spoiled. My parents praised me often. I followed the rules and was obedient and reasonable. I did what my parents told me to do because I considered their advice and opinions to be sound and the best for me. I didn't question them. It didn't occur to me that they could ever be wrong.

Oftentimes, I felt lonely in Lima. Being an introvert, I had few friends. I didn't have relatives from my mother's side of the family. Her father did not acknowledge his paternity and therefore, was never present for her or for me and my brother. My maternal grand-mother passed away when my mother was a little child, so I didn't get to meet her, either. Because my grandparents were never present, I was not aware of their absence until I was old enough to notice that my classmates had grandparents and I didn't know any of mine except for my adoptive grandmother. Only my father had a family. A large one. But they lived hundreds of miles away, in Puno, the Lake Titicaca city.

When I was seven, we finally went to visit. We stayed with our relatives for two weeks, and I had the time of my life. All of a sudden, I was surrounded by loving aunts and uncles who went out of their way to make sure I was happy and I enjoyed my stay. Aunts cooked elaborate special meals, and uncles took us on trips to the countryside and organized family get-togethers to celebrate our visit. I remember the first morning at their home as if it were yesterday. As I woke up, I saw many children standing around my bed in silence looking at me with curiosity. I couldn't tell how many there were! Soon, I was playing—running and laughing with them, coming up with strange kinds of culinary creations such as lettuce and candy sandwiches. Our creation! Together! I had a big family! I felt so happy to have met them, finally. They were my treasure. From that moment on, I felt, I would not be lonely again. I had a big loving family.

Even though I didn't see them again for seventeen years, the memory of what it felt like being surrounded by my beautiful family stayed with me. I had few friends and didn't feel like I fit in at elementary or high school. I was different—I didn't come from a wealthy background like my classmates, and my parents weren't professionals. I was the daughter of immigrants from the Andes, which, to my classmates, meant that I was at a lower level socially.

Being rejected was an everyday experience for me. I felt inferior and my self-esteem suffered. At the same time, this experience gave me the opportunity to learn at an early age to value my Andean cultural background. I didn't yet have a good understanding of the depth of my uniqueness and, at the same time, my connection to the people around me, my Inca ancestors and humanity.

It was so sad to see my father in his early forties, looking for a new job, and for months being told that he was too old to get any job. The only way out, my parents decided, was to invest the little savings they had in my father's trip to North America to find a job and a new life for all of us. And so, at age fifteen, I said goodbye to my father as he left Peru to look for a better life for us in North America. When he left, I felt as if I had a deep hole in my heart. I didn't know when I would see him again. His was a one-way ticket, and we all knew it. He held back tears; we all did. My mother and I smiled to give him courage as he got into the taxi that would take him to the airport.

In the following days… weeks… months, my mother and I cried often, trying not to let each other notice and wanting to keep a brave facade. My brother seemed to be calmer and less emotional about our father's absence. I don't remember ever seeing him cry about it, but it affected him much more than we knew; he became quieter and much more isolated.

Four years after my father's departure, he had settled in Vancouver, Canada, and was ready for us to join him. I was so excited that we would finally be together again! But even once we were together, I felt distance between us—after all, we had been apart for so long. Eventually, we all adapted and became a family again in our new surroundings. I admired my mother's determination and courage to start working right away, once we arrived. She was mindful that her husband's paycheck would not be enough to support a family of four. Two weeks after we arrived in Vancouver, she started working at a produce store without knowing any English. A coworker helped with translation when he could.

My mother, brother, and I went to English-as-a-second-language classes. I enjoyed going to class and meeting people from around the world. I found learning about their cultures fascinating. I made quick progress as I was so determined to learn English as soon as possible to communicate better and to prepare for a career. Growing up, I had been taught by my family and society that going to university and having a career meant leaving behind poverty, ensured a job (which was especially scarce in Peru at that time), brought respect from others, and paved the way for a higher social status and a comfortable lifestyle. Even with all of that, I wanted more—I truly desired to help people. I didn't know how, but I knew that I wanted to make a difference in the lives of people. I had a deep longing to be of service.

The first person I needed to help was my own brother, who had been behaving strangely and had an emotional crisis. I took him to an appointment with a psychologist. That day, I was told my brother had schizophrenia. Growing up, we didn't get along, but I loved my brother. I was in such shock when I was told of his diagnosis that I felt like I was out of my body, floating out there in emptiness except for the word "schizophrenia", which I heard echoing over and over again in my mind.

He started treatment, but medications didn't seem to work all that well. He was still hearing voices, his mood was altered, and he was so sleepy that he spent most of the time lying in bed. He became depressed and I had to take him to the hospital emergency room numerous times until he was hospitalized for three months in a psychiatric ward.

Soon, in one of my classes, I met the man who would later become my husband. He was an immigrant from the Middle East—a man with a big heart, who was caring and smart, someone who I admired and could trust. In the middle of this big city and new life I had found my best friend and someone who would take care of me. At age nineteen, I still felt like a child and my parents treated me as such—"for my own good." Later, I realized that my fiancé represented more of a father-figure who would take care of me and save me from my insecurity. Seven years after we started dating, we were engaged. Only then did I have the opportunity to see my family in Peru again.

Finding my way back to my heart sanctuary was not easy. I had learned at an early age to forget the path to my heart. I knew only how to live from my head. I had allowed my logical mind to be in charge of my life. You see, the problem I had was that my mind was listening to and believing all the internal and external voices telling me what I "should" do.

The voice of my own heart had been silenced for many years until I was finally brought to my knees. I had gotten married, but I did not really love my husband. Instead, guilt and

feelings of responsibility for his happiness took over. In truth, I was rejecting my one true soulmate— *my cousin*. I had battled with my feelings for him believing that our relationship was wrong, shameful, impossible, and illogical.

A few months before I got married, I graduated with a degree in nursing. I would work for seven long years in that field, feeling completely inadequate and burdened with terrible self-esteem. I didn't realize it then, but I had chosen a career based on my logical thinking: nurses were in high demand, paid well, and had the opportunity to serve people in a meaningful way.

My two biggest life decisions—getting married and becoming a nurse—were made from my head, for the most part, and not in sync with the beat of my own heart. And the consequences were so painful. The day after I separated from my husband, I cried, lying on the sofa feeling like a train had run me over and I was still alive to feel the pain. My body and soul hurt. I not only mourned the death of my marriage but also the loss of my whole family, as my parents and extended family judged me and condemned me harshly for separating from my husband and for being in love with my cousin.

"I no longer have a daughter," my mother told me, before I left the city for three years and disappeared from her. "You are dead."

My father called me a slut and a whore. While he screamed insults, my soul came out of my body to protect me. I could only hear him talk as if from a distance. Somehow, I could not really listen to those words. I found myself in a deep void, a parallel world of stillness. I could not feel emotions at that moment. I could not have tolerated them.

For the next three years, the depression I had been silently suffering from for years became severe. I also suffered from anxiety, post-traumatic stress disorder, a gluten sensitivity, allergies, and a skin condition called rosacea. At the root of all my pain and struggles, I was living from my head and allowing my ego to lead the way, rather than living from my heart sanctuary. My depression was at its worst during the years I "disappeared" from my family's life. I don't know how I made it to work and carried on with my nursing

121

duties in the isolated rural village where I went to live. I dragged myself from my bed to the sofa and cried often, mourning the death of the relationship with my family. I thought of my ex-husband often with deep sadness for him. The last thing I wanted was to hurt him, to destroy his dreams of having a family with me, to cause him suffering. Yet, I had torn his world apart, and I felt guilty. I carried the heavy weight of feeling responsible for his feelings. Through the worst of times, I told myself that one day I would be happy again. I prayed for that day to come. Feeling lonely in my empty apartment, the memories of my angry parents telling me that they were ashamed of me and all my relatives turning their backs on me haunted me day and night.

Fortunately, I had the gift of time. I spent hours thinking of them, what they did, what they said—and as I tried to understand them, I understood their pain and why my decisions and feelings had hurt them so much. My separation and divorce caused them to feel so much anger and resentment. Although the way in which my parents and my relatives reacted was devastating to me, I empathized with them and I forgave them quickly—although not completely. There was still a part of me that was wounded with anger and resentment. I wanted to forgive them much more. I desired to live in peace and be happy. How could I do it if I carried so much anger and resentment in me? How could I enjoy life while feeling so guilty?

The nightmare that had become my life was over when I began to align with my inner heart sanctuary and go back to my essence.

One day, two large eagles landed on my balcony. I stood there staring at them through the thin window pane just 3 meters away. One of them looked into my eyes, and as I was looking into his eyes time seemed to stop…those precious seconds of soul-to-soul meaningful connection with an eagle would stay with me forever. I knew that what had just happened was a significant event in my life, but I didn't know why. At the time, I wasn't aware that in the First Nations tradition, Grandfather Eagle is known as the messenger of Divine Spirit.

But, that wasn't all. Within a week I got another message from Divine Spirit that was impossible to ignore.

One morning, I had a vivid dream that I was walking down a park path when I suddenly stopped in fear. In front of me there was an alligator hiding behind a mound of soil ready to attack me. My soulmate was with me and encouraged me to keep walking. He held my hand, and we continued walking down the path. When I stepped on the mound of soil, the alligator attacked me. It bit my left hand and wouldn't let go of me. I avoided looking at my hand and the alligator hanging from it as I was walking. Finally, when we crossed the street, the alligator let go. I was sure I was bleeding and badly wounded, but when I looked at my left hand all I saw were superficial indentation marks that disappeared completely within seconds. I had not been harmed. I woke up feeling shaken by this dream. But I knew right away that the dream reflected the fear and anxiety I was living with every day and that despite how painful the present was, I would not be harmed permanently. *I would be okay.*

I got up and opened my Bible to a random page. I felt strongly that there was a message for me, something I needed to know. To my surprise, the Bible passage (Acts 28: 1 – 10) I laid my eyes on had an amazing resemblance to my life at that moment and the dream I had just woken up from. This passage told the story of a man who arrived on a boat to an island where the native people received him. He and the natives sat around a bonfire to talk and didn't notice that it got very late. In the darkness they could not see that a snake had come close to them and bit the visitor on the right hand. The native people were sure he would die because he had being bitten by the most venomous snake in the island and anyone who had being bitten by the snake had died. This man not only lived, he gained the ability to heal with his hands and healed many others.

This story connected with my life and my dream in interesting ways: I was living in a native island in Canada, and I had being bitten by a lizard on the hand in my dream that same morning. I was a nurse at the time helping people heal from physical illnesses. The message I received at that moment through the Bible passage was that all the pain and hardship I was going through in my life wouldn't kill me. I would receive a gift that was hidden in the pain and hardship. I would gain the ability to assist in many people's healing not as a nurse but in a new way. Later on, it was revealed to me that I was being called to rediscover my Inca High Priestess identity and myself as a divine healing channel to assist in the healing of women and humanity.

Shortly after my encounter with the eagles and these other revelations, I was guided to teachers and mentors who introduced me to a spiritually conscious life and encouraged me to go back to my roots as a source of healing. At the same time, a new synchronicity emerged. I started to notice that one after another, women who were Reiki practitioners showed up in my life. For more than thirty years I had not known about any kind of energy work at all or heard about Reiki, and then, all of a sudden, Reiki, an ancient healing modality of the lying on of hands was reappearing.

This was another synchronistic sign that I needed to pay attention to, so I began intentionally working on healing my life.

After some time, I traveled from Canada to Peru to marry my soulmate. After our wedding, we traveled to Cusco, the center of the ancient Incan Empire, to embark on a spiritual quest. For the first time in our lives, we immersed ourselves in our spiritual ancestral Inca ceremonies. I had forgotten them for so long. However, sitting on the countryside among the Andean mountains, deep into prayer invoking Pachamama (Mother Earth), the Apukunas (Spirits of the Mountains) and the Divine, in sacred Inca ceremonies, I attained deep peace and experienced bliss for the first time in life.

My whole being returned to alignment in the essence of love.

My soul danced in harmony with Pachamama and reunited with the souls of the wise Incas. As our sacred ceremony reached its highest point, I could feel their powerful yet sweet presence. Suffering and heartbreak paved the way back to my heart, back to my roots. And my soul persevered, leading me back to the Great Divine Spirit, the divinity in me, in you, and in every being.

About the Author

JESSICA CORNEJO GALLEGOS

Jessica Cornejo Gallegos is an Inca High Priestess, Shamanic Healer Guide and Heart Purpose Mentor. She is the founder of Alturas Shining Light Spiritual Journeys. Through her divinely inspired private healing services (spiritual * energetic * psychological), group programs and public speaking, she guides women to step into the light of their lives.

Jessica leads groups on sacred retreats to the land of the Incas, Cusco-Peru. Born in Peru and a Canadian citizen, she is a Reiki Master with a BSN degree and 7 years of nursing experience.

Years ago, Jessica experienced a depression and life crisis that led her to a spiritual awakening. Through synchronicities, she was guided by Spirit to transform her own life. She experienced profound leaps in her personal and spiritual development by participating in Inca's ceremonies during pilgrimages to Peru to be the High Priestess and wise spiritual guide and healer she is today.

Today, Jessica is the owner of Alturas Kitchen, a holistic restaurant in Cusco-Peru where she has been inspired to nourish people's bodies and souls. Jessica is currently providing life healing services and mentoring awakening women determined to transform their lives. Her commitment is to support women to transform their lives and experience a blissful purposeful life by aligning with their hearts, Pachamama and Spirit.

Learn More: **www.alturasshininglight.com**
Sign up for a Discovery Session here: **www.timetrade.com/book/YP2DC**
Email Jessica at **Jessica@alturasshininglight.com**

PHOTO BY ALEXANDER ESTRADA

Chapter 9

THE VOICE OF THE INNER ORACLE: LISTEN AND THRIVE

BY JULIE MCAFEE

Welcome! I am so glad you have found your way to these pages.

As a mom of three kids, a wife, a friend, a daughter, a sister, and a mentor for women, I understand how it feels to be overwhelmed and fighting your way to the surface just to keep your head above water. In this lifetime, it feels like I have been through hell and back—and I've been able to come out the other side, into the light.

Yes, I am an Oracle. As an oracle, I stand in my power—grounded—giving others support and permission to do the same.

I would best define Oracle, or the High Priestess, as someone who holds the highest vision of herself and embodies her gifts with amazing grace and confidence. She expresses her gifts to the world with love, light, gratitude, compassion—and a deep desire to serve others.

This is why I am here—to share my journey as a modern-day oracle of sacred soul wisdom. Wisdom that is inside you right now. Wisdom that you can access if you just say yes.

My life today is deeply fulfilling. I am so happy and grateful to be sharing the work and the gifts I have always known were meant to be used to serve the planet during this time of great transformation. I have created a truly blessed reality, with my husband and three vibrant and well-loved kids, in the beautiful mountains of Telluride, Colorado. I have deep passion for my one-on-one coaching work with clients from around the world, and for hosting regular women's retreats where I assist women in activating their inner wisdom.

I consciously live my life with grace, compassion, and intention, and as a witness to the work being done every day—and teach others to do the same. This life is very different than my previous life, before I had tapped into my own oracle wisdom.

In fact, there were many times in my teens and twenties in which my soul chose to have the experience of giving away my inner authority, power, and wisdom. I made dangerous and scary decisions that were not in alignment with my highest self.

Even just five years ago, I hit a rock-bottom moment! Coming from a background as a real-estate agent earning six-figures, I fell into shame as my family went through the most financially challenging phase we had ever experienced. At my lowest point, I found myself looking for change in between car seats to buy groceries…

And then, it got worse. I found out I was pregnant—completely unplanned. I thought, "How will I be able to take care of another child with so much fear and lack in my life?!" I was drowning in the shame of not feeling capable of taking care of another child, and was thrust back into my old conditioned patterns of fear, overwhelm, survival, terror, and disbelief that the universe had my back. I even had a friend anonymously donate groceries and children's clothing in front of my door, with money tucked into the clothing pockets. I couldn't believe this was my life. What had happened?

Miraculously, through a series of Theta Healings, I began to find my way back—to my self. I discovered my own sacred soul wisdom.

What is sacred soul wisdom?

Discovering your sacred soul wisdom means opening up to your highest truth and finding an elegance of grace. It means bringing joy and abundance into your life while removing fear, struggle, and beliefs that no longer serve you. It means finally living your life with passion, purpose, and love.

The process is one of stepping into your "gifts" and befriending your higher self, your truth, and your power. It is a journey of evolution—an ascension process—that may create some fear because it is so new to your experience. At a cellular level, your body is shifting and changing very fast. You may feel resistance, confusion, or even sickness.

If you are feeling a calling deep in your heart, I want you to know that there is a special knowledge that awaits to be woken up so you can expand more deeply in all areas of your life.

I am here to let you know there are many of us going through this, and you are not alone! You will be okay, and I am here to guide you. This is powerful beyond belief! Connecting with your soul's essence and allowing your soul's wisdom to flower is the most beautiful experience imaginable. Trust this.

In this new paradigm, I am showing you what it feels like to step into your truth and power and activate the innate wisdom and knowledge that you hold. I am the witness to the work being done so that you can live in your passion and purpose.

By listening to the voice of your inner oracle, you will will be filled with more confidence, love, joy, abundance, gratitude and purpose. You will feel like a new person!

Let's take a look at how you can access your sacred soul wisdom and listen to your Oracle.

THE KEY CORNERSTONES OF CONSCIOUSNESS

Step 1: Release
Step 2: Clear
Step 3: Receive

Many of us have given up our free will—our "right to choice"—by allowing our unconscious mind, ego, and other people to inadvertently create our beliefs and life situation for us.

So the first step in this process of raising your consciousness is to **release** the old belief systems. By this, I mean to surrender to your higher self, to let go of all your old stories—delete the old files, so to speak, and rewrite the code of your life.

When you make the decision to release and step into your truth and power, your life will shift by leaps and bounds. You will experience more freedom. You will have clarity on your intentions and more confidence overall. In short, you will learn how to create the life of your dreams.

By becoming conscious of your choices, you take back your truth and live a deeper, more expansive level of existence. You begin to step into your power every day as you release the old and make room for the new. It is a feeling, a knowing, a deeply rooted wisdom that is ready to blossom and be in the light. The more you become familiar with this feeling, the more you will stand in your power. You will notice things coming into your life that you wished for and opportunities will show up, or perhaps your family, personal, and business life will improve. Your vision will begin to manifest into reality.

This power is not the power of the ego but rather your truth—an ancient knowledge that you hold in your heart. It is your soul's wisdom, your soul's essence. Once you have made the decision to release the old belief systems, courage and elegance begin to take form. You will enjoy experiencing it. In fact, most of my clients feel it in the first session.

The second step is to **clear** the old beliefs that no longer serve you. These beliefs have built up and manifested into the physical and emotional body and may have served you for one reason or another. Sometimes the emotional baggage will layer into your physical body and create sickness. For example, sickness may serve some underlying, subconscious need to create more support for yourself by bringing your family together.

Here is how it works. You clear, clear, clear, and release what no longer serves you. The programs in your subconscious mind create the life you have and attract specific people, experiences, and events to you. This includes the negative, limiting beliefs, and struggles that may be hindering you from living your dreams.

Did you know that the subconscious mind governs 88 percent of the brain, while the conscious mind governs only 12 percent?

Have you ever asked yourself, "Why is this happening to me again?" or "Why have I attracted this into my life?" In short, the limiting belief systems and programs stored in your subconscious mind win over the conscious mind every time.

These limiting beliefs in our subconscious are not only learned from childhood (from this lifetime) but are also stored in our DNA (at least two generations old), group collective consciousness (not even your baggage), and the soul level. Once you shake these beliefs free from the bondage in your mind, your ego fades and you feel lighter and clearer, with more compassion and gratitude in your heart.

Once you clear out the limiting belief systems and the thoughts that aren't serving you, you're ready to **receive**. Now that you have removed these veils of beliefs, you are able to tap into your inner wisdom and knowledge with ease and grace, thereby consciously creating your reality and visions. You become more spacious to receive support, resources, and love. You begin to receive the blessings that God has to offer you.

When I finally began to receive in my life, I stopped judging myself and other people, and I noticed an increasing amount of compassion for myself and for others. I also began to feel a deep relationship with animals, and a deepening connection with the earth, nature, and the elements. I now have a relationship with my angels, higher self, and guides from many different realms. I am filled with more kindness, presence, and purpose because I feel the connection with everything and everyone. Sometimes just smiling at a person on the street, or sitting with an elderly person and taking the time to ask them how they are doing makes all the difference in the world.

Now it is a gift to serve, whereas in the past it felt like work, constantly trying to prove myself to *me*, which was a heavy energy…what a struggle!

Now, my surroundings reflect my inner truth and the people I attract are the people I am here to serve, be present with and co-create with the magnificent shifts that are taking place here on earth.

Now, I am in my highest and best state, connected with my divine purpose in service and reflecting the same to others.

Release, clear, receive.

This is the path of the priestess that I walk on. Come, I'll show you the way.

About the Author

JULIE MCAFEE

The path to Julie's temple winds up and around a lush hilltop, with portals of ascension and sacred spaces to stop, reflect and transform. In the glow of iridescent white, Julie awaits at the top of the final staircase, holding the space of transformation for those brave enough to say yes to life. You have arrived. It is here, in the Sacred Temple of Wisdom and Knowledge, where gathering and sisterhood bring forth the healing that is needed.

Inside this temple of light are secrets and answers to the questions you seek. Julie is the keeper of the magic, holding power and connection, moving seamlessly between here and now and the energy of the Universe that flows through her. This space is the sacred container for Julie's clients, an energetic frame for healing, clearing and finally ascending beyond the static and nonsense noise of the Matrix towards the magic of Source. Julie supports many with the reawakening of their internal light and gifts, through DNA activations, ThetaHealing® Modality, pineal gland clearing, and reprograming the subconscious to awaken to their truth.

Internationally acclaimed, Julie is known for supporting female leaders in empowerment and embodiment of the feminine. She is complex—a swirl of light energy and the divine feminine undulating like the rising Kundalini snake—open to infinite information, guidance and truth, holding the door for other ascendant beings. Her method is simple—clear your field of the negative, and fill your soul with light and love.

One of Julie's greatest gifts is assisting people to remove the veils of fear, limiting beliefs, releasing old programs and patterns that no longer serve them. They begin to trust and re-awaken their intuitive intelligence, ancient knowledge, wisdom and inner knowing. Opening the doors to their gifts and celebrating the embodiment of their souls essence (the ascension process), they now have a clear pathway for abundance, and the tools to consciously create their dreams, fully love and be of service in the world with purpose.

Join her at one of her events, retreats, classes or one-on-one sessions. Learn More: **www.JulieMcAfee.com** or email **julie.mcafee@gmail.com.**

Chapter 10

THE PREGNANT PAUSE:
SURRENDER INTO PURE POTENTIALITY

BY SOFIAH THOM

When I was 15 my father told me; "If you are going to have sex, you have to think about God, and if you don't you will fuck yourself."

Here I sit almost 25 years later, edging on 40, desiring to have a baby, and looking back on my life and how this one comment left an imprint that shaped my relationship with myself and my sexuality.

I desire to be a mother, to have a baby, and I am thinking of God—being with God in this process—and every moon that comes I have to let go and surrender again and again into trust.

Let me share my story of how I have learned to BE in this place of trust and surrender. I call this place of deep surrender the Pregnant Pause—it's the space between breaths, the deep mystery, the fertile void where pure potentiality lives.

Growing up I was always fascinated with sex. I spent hours entranced with pictures I'd collected—obsessed with bodies and sexuality—confused and ashamed and excited. My late teens were defined by a rich sexual tapestry.

My walk with sacred sex led me to dance, and I learned to see my body as a temple, my expression and unique essence sacred. While studying Dance Therapy I learned to love myself first, and honor my body and the sacred intimacy and divine connection to something greater than myself.

I was fascinated with the history of Temple Dancers from India and wondered how I could bring Sacred Sexuality and Temple Dance into our modern culture now. I recognized how our bodies are our temples and that we must honor our bodies, our expression, and our intimacy with others. It is essential to love ourselves first and foremost and to see our bodies and unique essence as sacred. Our expression through our temple body is how we show our devotion to something greater than ourselves. After graduating in Dance Therapy when I was 24, I followed a dream and desire to dive deeper into the art of Temple dance and went on a solo pilgrimage to India.

Here in the temples of India and at the Odissi Dance School, I experienced deep intuition within myself that I already carried this devotional temple dance within my DNA. I simply had to surrender and allow myself to be moved by this awakening, and I realized that one of my gifts is to help women remember their essence and their devotion to the great mystery through their dance.

Going back to everyday life in London was a struggle after the rich smorgasbord of India, and I felt completely lost—like a stranger, disconnected from my passion and purpose…until one day I found my self in the right place—an audition with Martin and the Limon company—and said yes to the next big curve in my path: The Tamalpa Institute for Expressive Healing Arts.

After my first visit with Anna and Daria Halprin at the Institute, I knew with every cell that this was a YES! I spent a year at Tamalpa going deep into the myths and stories held in my body. I uncovered the belief systems that were not mine and had been placed onto me by my family, my culture, and the world. I reclaimed my sovereignty and allowed myself to be seen for the fullness of who I was. I spent the next five years teaching, performing and working one-on-one through bodywork, dance and expressive healing arts. I built a following and supported myself doing what I loved.

In my late 20's, I had a vision of moving to Los Angeles where my work would explode. I quickly followed my intuition and immediately landed a job at the premier LA yoga studio where everything seemed to fall into place magically. I found myself in the most happening and spiritually evolved, embodied community, filled with yoga and dance and all of the things I loved. For the first time, I felt like I had arrived in a place where my inner desires and gifts were being reflected and celebrated through abundance in my outer life. My work was booming and so was my bank account. It felt truly wonderful to be in LA with so much possibility for growth. I had found my community and place in the world.

As everything was falling perfectly into place in my dream LA world, I was invited to a high-end, exclusive New Years Retreat in Ojai as a guest massage therapist. On New Years Eve I created a ritual where I threw a dragonfly into the fire to release any illusions about my life and my current relationship that I had been trying to leave for awhile.

Then something terrible happened. At the end of this retreat I received a massage as a gift. The moment I saw the therapist a little voice inside me told me that I shouldn't go ahead with the massage. But my mind told my body that I deserved it, so I ignored my inner warnings. That decision changed the course of my life as I knew it.

I barely walked away from that massage. An incorrect adjustment of my neck left me with two herniated discs and nerve pain down my arms and into my hands. My world unraveled before my eyes. How would I teach? How would I do bodywork? I limped away like a wounded animal as my world came crashing down around me. I felt like the rug had been pulled out from underneath me and I was left in an empty room with no doors and nowhere to go.

Not only did I get injured, I lost my identity and direction. Who was I without my body and without my health? How would I survive? And who would even care in this strange city of Los Angeles?

From one moment to the next I went from dreamland to lost, depressed, scared, broke and in pain. My flexibility and my sexual creative nature had been robbed from me and I couldn't move. I blamed the masculine for all the oppression on women and felt a direct experience of this in my body and in my limited dark world.

I couldn't understand why everything that I had been building and thought I wanted was suddenly taken away from me, and I spiraled into a down-cycle of self-pity and remorse.

I became dependent on pain medications, my cash was running out and I just kept asking myself, "Why me? Why is this terrible thing happening to me? Is this my punishment for how free I have been with my sexuality?" I lost my friends, my boyfriend, my clients, and my community. I questioned everything. I hit rock bottom with no purpose, no direction and was left feeling utterly alone.

After months and endless nights of feeling lost and down in self-pity and shame, I realized I had to do something really brave and make a huge shift—I had to take charge of my situation and my life in a new way! This was an opportunity to practice what I preach and journey into my painbody to find the wisdom living within. It was time to regain the trust in my inner voice and innate wisdom. My mind had overridden my inner voice before which led me to this deeply painful situation and now it was time to heal and remember the wisdom living within.

I dug down deep inside, deeper than the pain, deeper than my fears and deeper than my self-pity. I realized my life was guiding me to let go of EVERYTHING I identified with, and that was the scariest thing I had ever done. My body's wisdom and my inner voice helped me to gather my strength and say YES to letting go and carving a new path. This meant going far, far away from everyone and everything I knew.

I swallowed my self-pity and reached out to one of my earliest mentors Melissa Michaels for help, and despite my injury, she invited me to assist her in a five rhythms retreat in New Zealand.

I felt myself saying YES without knowing how I would do it. I had no money, but some part of me knew that this was what my body and spirit needed. I took a chance and asked one of my old clients to help me buy a plane ticket to go on this spiritual quest, and I was off! I said yes to the unknown with a sense of trust and entered into the Pregnant Pause.

The Pregnant Pause—the space between breaths, the mysterious fertile void where anything is possible and where pure potentiality lives.

The next six months birthed many beautiful movements out of the Pregnant Pause. I learned to trust myself again by listening to my inner voice and allowing it to guide me. I fell in love with the musician from the retreat and created the music of my soul. I tapped into my artistic creativity

and channeled spirit songs that brought me back to my roots. I was able to go deep into my body and clear the shame and sadness I was carrying. I channeled my shakti—my creative sexual energy—and accessed my creative potential through my authentic voice.

I birthed two songs out of the Pregnant Pause, called *Soul Calling* and *Remembrance*. By singing these songs I remembered my soul's calling and the wisdom passed down through my ancestry. As I created and sang, I remembered my inner strength and courage once again as a spiritual warrior and was filled with gratitude for the family I was born into.

You see, I was born into a very special family. I was raised fourth generation Subud, an international spiritual movement with a core philosophy and practice that focuses on opening to the divine force within each of us. Singing helped me to remember my lineage and access this divine creative life force that naturally wants to move through me.

I also recognized at this time that my creative, spiritual and sexual power comes from the same source, so as I channeled this strong creative current I learned the importance of containing this energy and to discern who I shared it with and how.

It was in New Zealand where I got to explore this discernment through the power of my sexuality in relationship to others. Through experiences and relationships I got to see myself as a wisdom teacher, holding the gift of the temple priestess and sacred sexuality through my creative expression and beingness.

When I returned home from New Zealand I was invited to teach The Art of Orgasm with my former client and friend, Michael Pooley. These teachings came directly from one of the books from my childhood bookshelf obsessions. It was an incredible full circle experience and gift in reclaiming my sexuality and truly surrendering any residual shame.

Teaching with Michael was my initiation into greater depths of sacred sexuality and my work. I felt like I had found myself again and my path was opening up. Now I had an understanding of my new gifts and how to move forward but I still didn't know how to support myself financially on this new found path.

It was around this time that I was invited to a wedding for two people who I actually had introduced when I was in India six years prior.

While there, I met my beloved and mentor Brendan.

I saw a tall, dark and handsome man with a big smile placing beautiful Balinese parasols on the land. I went over to him weak at the knees to introduce myself. The first thing he said to me is, "Are you *the* Sofiah?" I replied, "I guess so…" and we quickly realized we had already been connected through a mutual friend.

At this wedding, my worlds came together. Many characters from different periods of my life were gathered together to celebrate. I offered a dance for the bride and groom and when Brendan saw me dance, he tasted my essence, and immediately believed in me and my art.

This wedding truly symbolized my soul family and tribe opening its arms to me after I had bravely let go of everything I knew. As soon as I met Brendan and he shared his world with me, I knew he was part of my dream. I immediately felt I was supposed to move to Costa Rica where he lived and co-create a life with him. Brendan quickly became my mentor. He helped me understand that I didn't need to see the world in a conventional way, that I could think as big as I wanted, and that my duty to myself and the world lay in actually marrying my spirituality with financial success.

So I took the leap into the mystery once again.

I moved to Costa Rica to build a dream—my healing arts retreat center. Now I was thinking big and outside the box, and it was a success! My lifetime of teachings and trainings, from my spiritual heritage, my healing, my trials and everything I had learned up to that point, came together to create a successful business aligned with my life's calling. I went from not having any money to building and opening a retreat center with my beloved in less than year.

During the next two years I proposed to my beloved and we co-created the wedding of our dreams which planted the seed and birthed Envision Festival, a Transformational festival focusing on Music, Art and Sacred Movement, in our back yard. Envision helped to put our town in the Southern zone of Costa Rica on the map and bring thousands of like-minded people to our area.

One night after returning home from five months on tour teaching and performing, my neck went out and I woke up unable to move. Even though it was extremely hard to swallow the truth of what my body was telling me, I immediately knew my body was communicating with me to guide me into yet another Pregnant Pause and so I surrendered, listened and carved a new way.

I deeply wanted a baby—this desire was living in me when I moved to Costa Rica. However, instead of getting pregnant, I channeled this energy into creating my retreat center Danyasa, and then creating Envision Festival. Now here I was—seven years later—still wanting a baby, but with no space to create. I knew I had to change how I was working and living.

I spent the next five months being in stillness; writing, learning to love myself more and practicing sustainability through my actions. I went deep into the pain and learned how to discover the gems from the dark cave of my existence. I realized I simply could not rely solely on my body for work anymore—my body and spirit were asking for more, guiding me into another level of my work. I began to put myself and my teachings out there through my words, sharing my wisdom online through webinars and tele-courses.

I knew I needed to practice a deep level of self love every day in order to be truly successful and create the space in my life to move into motherhood. In order to do this, we had to clear the pathway and create space which meant letting go of more. And so, Brendan and I decided to bow out of producing Envision, and focus on our family and our own personal work. Letting go of Envision was like letting go of my baby! After putting so much of my creative energy, blood, sweat and tears into it, it physically hurt me to let go and surrender once again into the unknown…

And so I passed the torch.

There was yet another wave that came to uproot my husband and I from Costa Rica. Seven years after birthing my retreat center, I received a clear message to support my husband. Two weeks after this message came, Brendan and I were having a visioning weekend together, where he shared his deep desire to get out of his comfort zone. Living his YES was to spread his wings, leave Costa Rica, explore, and support me in my work. As I listened to his desire I felt every cell of my body saying YES, this is what it looks like to support Brendan. His YES looked like leaving Costa Rica after 25 years of being rooted there.

So we let go of the reins and surrendered again into the unknown and into the Pregnant Pause together.

Today, I am in the unknown, in the deep mystery, in the dark underbelly and yet, from my life experience and from my connection to source, I have learned that the only way through is to fully surrender, let go and trust. I sit here in my desire, my deep desire, to conceive a child.

We have been calling this in for over two years now and still it has not come. When I sit with myself in the stillness, I feel and know the truth of my life's path—it is perfect in its divine unfolding. For if I had already given birth to a baby, I would not have had the space to rebirth myself again and again. I feel that a baby is waiting to come through me. I have done my best to listen during this Pregnant Pause and connect with this spirit baby. My sense is that the spirit of the baby knows exactly when to come through and is helping to clear the pathway and allow space to come through.

Almost everyday, I am faced with society's and other people's pressure and belief system that fertility at my age is dangerous, but this belief system encroaches on my innate wisdom. YES, I am approaching 40, and NO, I will not freeze my eggs. Standing in my power and inner knowing is crucial to this process of the Pregnant Pause. I fully trust in the divine timeline happening in every moment that we cannot see, but only believe. I am deep in the gestation period of my next creation, like a butterfly in its cocoon, patiently loving myself and trusting in the process.

Everything that happens is a lesson—a gift—and so I sit here in the unknown in the Pregnant Pause, surrendering and trusting and allowing my life to unfold. Giving birth is another expression of our beautiful sexuality—this thread of sacred sexuality is a pillar of who I am and the work I am here to do. I know that having a baby will bring my work to the next level, and so I trust in all that transpires.

Trust in the mystery and open to divinity.

I know that every day is rich, the doors are opening and the mystery is unfolding. Following my YES is not necessarily an easy path, it requires full surrender and trust at all times. I have had to leave many things behind; lovers, friends, ventures and opportunities, which many people will call me crazy for. And yet, this path is about carving our own way, leading those ready to venture into the great mystery and discover their true gifts and purpose.

In order to say YES to our divine purpose we have to know how to discern, we have to know how to say no in order to say YES. This is the path of the priestess—to know oneself through listening, through remembering, through being.

The path of the priestess lies in the pregnant pauses between worlds, between form and formlessness. I listen and honor my Inner voice, my knowing, and my wisdom as I dance the path of the priestess, and know that we are powerful beyond measure. When we harness our sexual creative power, we can birth ourselves again and again through the evolution of being human in this world.

again and again we are asked to let go
to surrender what we thought we knew
to be open and receive
to trust in the unknown

to be
to birth again and again

to evolve
to upgrade
to remember
to believe in our own power
our innate wisdom

I bow to the deep mystery. I am a living prayer of gratitude.

Through this journey on the path of the priestess, I am grateful for all the teachings and for my parents for offering me the gift of seeing the marriage of sex and spirit from a very young age. May I bring this knowledge through, so that we can honor our sacred temple bodies, our sexuality and our souls' purpose on our unique path.

About the Author

SOFIAH THOM

Sofiah Thom lives to dance. Through sacred movement and creative expression, Sofiah exudes embodied wisdom that effortlessly inspires others to connect with their deepest purpose. Sofiah strives to be a vessel for divine spirit, that she might help others connect with their unique expression of creativity. She believes that every person possesses an inner artist—a unique, individual creative spark that just needs to be allowed or inspired to show itself. Sofiah's mission lies in nurturing this creative spark in others with the aim to inspire them to live to their fullest creative potential and create the life they dream of.

Sofiah's passion for the sacred healing arts stems from a lifetime journey of devotion. Sofiah is fourth generation Subud, the essence of which rests in supporting and honoring each practitioner's personal direct experience of spirit. Sofiah's lifelong personal practice in this tradition shines through clearly in her teaching and performance. She is a Goddess Coach and sacred movement artist, teacher and trainer as well as an online coach and mentor. Sofiah teaches and performs at festivals and events globally, where she inspires conscious connection and inspiration through her dance and performances.

Sofiah co-founded the Envision Festival in Costa Rica, a conscious festival celebrating music, art and sacred movement, and Danyasa Eco-Retreat, a center for wellness and transformative experience in the beautiful beach town of Dominical, Costa Rica, with a focus on creating unique and educational experiences that serve the personal needs, transformation, and growth.

Learn More: **www.sofiahthom.com, sofiah@sofiahthom.com, www.envisionfestival. com, www.danyasa.com.**

For more information, please visit us at

www.thepathofthepriestessbook.com

22963666R00093

Made in the USA
San Bernardino, CA
29 July 2015